NAZIM
HIKMET
POETRY
FESTIVAL

TO LIVE
LIKE A TREE
ALONE AND FREE
LIKE A FOREST
IN BROTHERHOOD

Organized By ATA-NC
Founded in 1987, **American Turkish Association of North Carolina (ATA-NC)** is a non-profit, member supported organization dedicated to promoting awareness of Turkish culture and sharing Turkish heritage throughout the state of North Carolina.
www.ata-nc.org

Hosted by Town of Cary

Additional Support Provided By
Jacar Press
Duke University Global Education Office for Undergraduates
NC Poetry Society

Festival Organizing Committee:
Buket Aydemir, Pelin Balı, Richard Krawiec, Mehmet C. Öztürk, Birgül Tuzlalı, and Ezgi Üstündağ

Cover Design: Pelin Balı

Tenth Annual
Nâzım Hikmet Poetry Festival

April 8, 2018 · Page-Walker Arts & History Center · Cary, NC

☙

Table of Contents

Foreword 1

About Nâzım Hikmet 4

Remembering Kathryn Stripling Byer 7

Buried Alive: Nâzım Hikmet's Afterlife Poems - Jill Stockwell 12

Nazim Hikmet: Harbinger of Hope - Greg Dawes 23

Nâzım Hikmet and The Poetics of Confinement - Erdağ Göknar 28

Nazim Hikmet: The Forms of Exile – Mutlu Konuk Blasing 37

Tenth Annual Nâzım Hikmet Poetry Competition 51

    Poetry Selection Committee 52

    Winners 53

        Peter Blair
        Michael Cirelli
        Laura Grothaus
        Rushda Rafeek
        Anya Russian
        Deema K. Shehabi

    Honorable Mentions 85

        Chris Abbate
        Jen Arthur
        Jill Coyle
        Maximilian Heinegg

Foreword

Few experiences are more satisfying to volunteers than seeing a cause to which they have devoted many long months—sometimes years—have an impact on a wider population. And for poetry lovers, there is nothing more satisfying than finding a community of writers and literature enthusiasts with which to discuss, dissect, and re-discover the wonders of this medium. We, as the organizers of the Nâzım Hikmet Poetry Festival, who are fortunate enough to wear both hats, have had the privilege of building community through poetry for the past decade.

What was, in 2008, a small gathering planned by a group of friends and lifelong admirers of the Festival's namesake has grown into a global competition and an annual staple of the Triangle literary scene. Over the past nine years, the Festival recognized and published more than 100 poets, representing a remarkably diverse cohort from many US states, different countries and ethnic backgrounds. Many of these poets joined us at the Festival to read their poems and enjoyed meeting other poets, publishers and poetry lovers.

Every year, the Festival also celebrates a poet of international renown through readings, panel discussions, presentations and musical performances. Some of our past featured poets include Pablo Neruda (Chile), Mahmoud Darwish (Palestine), Seamus Heaney (Ireland), Anna Akhmatova (Russia), Mevlana Celaleddin Rumi (Iran & Turkey), and Wisława Szymborska (Poland).

The Festival has initiated and completed several Turkish poetry translation projects, including the Divitçi Prize. Most recenty, Sidney Wade and Efe Murad received the 2014 Divitçi Prize for their translations of Melih Cevdet Anday. Their collection, *Silent Stones: Selected Poems of Melih Cevdet Anday* was recently published by Talisman House.

In the months leading up to the Festival, **Jacar Press** (one of our sponsors) organizes poetry and creative workshops with award-winning writers and artists that are held in the Turkish House in Cary, NC. The 30-40 slots available at each workshop frequently fill up far in advance!

To mark its tenth anniversary, the organizing committee has expanded the one-day event at Page-Walker Arts & History Center to span three days and three different venues around Cary: a concert at the Cary Arts Center, a workshop and film screening at the Cary Theater, and a day of readings and discussion at Page Walker Arts and History Center. We hope that these diverse activities have reached a larger audience and introduced some readers to Nâzım Hikmet.

No event can thrive for a decade without the involvement of several dedicated community partners. It is necessary to restate our gratitude for the **Town of Cary**'s unwavering commitment to the Festival through the Cultural Arts Funding grant program, as well as their assistance in securing facilities and logistical support. We would especially like to thank Mayor Harold Weinbrecht, Councilman Ken George, Councilman Jack Smith, Lyman Collins, Kris Carmichael and Jennifer Hocken.

The Festival could not have made the leap from enthusiastic discussions among friends to an annual event, drawing hundreds of attendees without the logistical and material support of the **American Turkish Association of North Carolina (ATA-NC)**, which has been our parent organization from the start.

Erdağ Göknar and the Duke University Middle East Studies Center have been instrumental in not only supporting the Festival's coordination but also reaching out to the academic community and helping the organizers to curate diverse and interesting keynote speakers and panels.

We are indebted to all judges of previous competitions. Without their dedicated work, it would not have been possible to run a successful competition for 10 years. Among our judges, we must single out Professor **Greg Dawes**, who served on the poetry selection committee of our competition for ten consecutive years.

This year's poetry selection committee included **Erdag Göknar, Greg Dawes** and **Rachel Richardson** as the final judges. We are grateful to them for their immense contribution to the festival.

We would like to thank our invited speaker, **Dr. Jill Stockwell** of Princeton University for joining us at the festival to give a talk on Nâzım Hikmet and his poetry. Her article, "Buried Alive: Nâzım Hikmet's Afterlife Poems" is included in this book along with three more articles by **Erdağ Göknar, Greg Dawes** and **Mutlu Konuk** published in previous years' books.

Finally, we would like to thank **you** for attending the current and past festivals. We could not have made it to year ten without your support!

Buket Aydemir, Pelin Balı, Richard Krawiec,
Mehmet C. Öztürk, Birgül Tuzlalı, Ezgi Üstündağ

About Nâzım Hikmet

Nâzım Hikmet, the foremost modern Turkish poet, was born in 1902 in Selânik. He grew up in Istanbul and was introduced to poetry early, publishing his first poems at the age of 17. He attended the Naval Academy but was discharged due to repeated bouts of pleurisy. Attracted by the Russian revolution and its promise of social justice, he crossed the border and made his way to Moscow and studied Political Science and Economics. He met the poet Vladimir Mayakovsky and other artists of the futurist movement and his style changed from Ottoman literary conventions to free verse.

He returned to Turkey in 1928 and spent five of the next ten years in prison on a variety of trumped-up charges due to his leftist views. During this time, he published nine books that revolutionized Turkish poetry and the Turkish language. In 1938, he was arrested for supposedly inciting the Turkish armed forces to revolt. He was sentenced to 28 years in prison on the grounds that military cadets were reading his poems. While in prison, he composed some of his greatest poems as well as his epic masterpiece *Human Landscapes from My Country*. He wrote a total of 66,000 lines; according to his letters, 17,000 of those survived.

In 1949, an international committee including Pablo Picasso, Paul Robeson and Jean Paul Sartre was formed in Paris to campaign for his release. In 1950 he was awarded the World Peace Prize, which Pablo Neruda accepted on his behalf. The same year he went on an 18-day hunger strike despite a recent heart attack and was released under the general amnesty of the newly elected government. Following his release, there were repeated attempts to murder him. He was followed everywhere. When he was ordered to do his military service at the age of fifty, he fled the country and was stripped of Turkish citizenship. His citizenship was officially restored by the Turkish government fifty-eight years later on January 5, 2009.

Nâzım Hikmet did not live to see his later poems published in Turkish, although they were translated into more than forty languages during his lifetime. He died of a heart attack in 1963, at the age of sixty-one. During the fifteen years after his death, his eight volume "Collected Poems", plays, novels and letters were gradually published.

Many celebrations of Nazim's 100th birthday took place in 2002: the Turkish Ministry of Culture sponsored several events; UNESCO named 2002 "The Year of Nâzım Hikmet"; and the American Poetry Review put him on their cover and published a collection of his poems.

Remembering Kathryn Stripling Byer

It is always difficult to identify a single individual who has been the most instrumental to the success of an initiative. In the case of the Nâzım Hikmet Poetry Festival, Kathryn Stripling Byer is this individual.

In early 2009, soon after articulating the concept of a poetry event to honor Nâzım Hikmet, we reached out to Kay, who was then the poet laureate of North Carolina. Her enthusiasm gave the organizing committee the encouragement and inspiration to execute a successful first Festival. That same year, her coverage of the competition on her website was instrumental in attracting submissions from many poets around the state of NC. Her monetary contribution to the festival helped us announce a group of winners rather than a single poet, a tradition that continues to this day, which we believe reflects the spirit of Nâzım. Kay also gifted us one of her poems to publish in the first Festival book, which we are including once again in this tenth anniversary edition.

After the first year, Kay continued to support us and served on the competition selection committee for many years. In 2013, we welcomed her as the Festival's invited poet. We are grateful and fortunate to have her as a friend and cannot thank her enough. Kay's spirit will always be with us.

Birgül, Buket, Mehmet and Pelin

"The celebration of Nâzım Hikmet's contribution to the world of poetry has become today a celebration of North Carolina poetry, as well. Bringing the two together has been one of the most important events I've witnessed since I became Laureate. Thanks to this festival, I have been introduced to Hikmet's poetry, and I have seen, as a judge of this year's contest, an amazing outpouring of poetry here in our state. Never before have I beheld such a splendid gathering of submissions to a poetry contest! Trying to choose among them was the most difficult task I've encountered as a judge. I congratulate the winners, all the poets who submitted their work, and the organizers of this festival. I am grateful to have been a part of this event. Thank you. "

- Kathryn Stripling Byer, NC Poet Laureate, 2005-2009
for the 2009 Festival

EACH MORNING
                Budapest, October, '08

"Today is Sunday. For the first time they took me out into the sun..."
      Nazim Hikmet, "Bugün Pazar"

Beneath the church
we saw each morning,
descending to breakfast,
lay ruins of a mosque,
perhaps tombs,
perhaps poems
buried under the foundation.

We climbed to Gul Baba's
crypt to find locks on the gate.
Roses clung to the fence
as if trying to reach us,
but nowhere could I find
a poem by the dead poet

unless it lay inside the petals
of each rose, like dreams
beneath eyelids.

We stood on the Margit Bridge
watching the Danube keep flowing.
We studied
the time-tables,
which trains to Istanbul,
which to Slovakia,
Bulgaria. Budapest glowed
in the sunset, an ancient
fire banked, embers pulsing
like quasars. Each morning
the sky opened
as to a captive released
after years of imprisonment.

Where had we been
all our lives? Had our eyes
become so used
to how the sun rose and set
over our homeland
that we had forgotten how sky

unfolds elsewhere? That words
not our own sing their
stories through alleys
and crowded streets?
Deserts of exile? Lying
at night in our four-star
hotel, I heard words
turn to flesh again,
I heard my heart beating,
(as if a jewel in my chest began
begging for safekeeping)
sounding its two unmistakable words,
this life,
this life.

Kathryn Stripling Byer (1944 -2017) was a passionate champion of poetry, environmentalism, civil rights, education, food pantries and other causes. After earning her M.F.A. from UNC Greensboro, where she studied under Allen Tate, Fred Chappell and Robert Watson, she taught for a decade at Western Carolina University as their poet-in-residence. She was the first woman to serve as North Carolina poet laureate (2005-2009). During her tenure, she created the blog My Laureate's Lasso, where she featured the work of other North Carolina poets. Her numerous awards include fellowships from the National Endowment for Arts and the N. C. Arts Council, and the North Carolina Award for Literature. She published nine books of poetry and was finishing a tenth when she died from complications related to lymphoma. Her full-length collections include The Girl in the Midst of the Harvest (AWP Award series), Wildwood Flower (Academy of American Poets Lamont Prize), Black Shawl, Catching Light, Coming to Rest (Hanes Award from Fellowship of Southern Writers) and Descent. The last five published by LSU Press. Her chapbooks are Wake, Southern Fictions, a hand letter-press Book Art featuring handmade paper covers, and the final book published in her lifetime, The Vishnu Bird (Jacar Press), a memorial and memoir of a close friend who died. In 2012, she was inducted into the NC Literary Hall of Fame.

Buried Alive: Nâzım Hikmet's Afterlife Poems

Jill Stockwell, Princeton University
March 2018

> *Will my funeral procession start from our courtyard?*
> *How will you carry me down from the third floor?*
> *There's no way the coffin will fit in the elevator,*
> *and the stairs are much too narrow.*

-- "My Funeral Ceremony," April 1963[1]

Near the end of his life, Turkish modernist poet Nâzım Hikmet Ran (1902-1963) often wrote about his death – or, more precisely about how the world would continue beyond it. Sometimes these poems are tinged with sadness, as in the case of "Days," in which he laments the inevitable end[2]:

> *Beautiful days in the future*
> *They won't see me*
> *At least let me send them my regards*
> *I'm dying of sorrow.*

In other poems, he attempts to shake off his thoughts of death and live fully the moment while he still can, as in an untitled poem that begins "I stripped off my thoughts of death/I donned the June leaves of the boulevard."[3] In a few rare verses, the poet indulges in gallows humour, as in the poem quoted above, "My Funeral Ceremony," in which he imagines all of the potential follies of the ceremonial procession. He humorously speculates about the awkward journey with the coffin down the narrow stairs of his apartment building, the curious children who would inevitably cluster gather around the body, and the pigeon who might leave a parting gift on his forehead.

Despite their varying tones, these poems share a pair of common themes that are central to Hikmet's work, namely, the constant

---

[1] All translations are my own. Nazım Hikmet Ran, "Cenaze Merasimim," *Bütün Şiirleri* (İstanbul: Yapı Kredi Yayınları, 2011): 1858.
[2] Ibid., 1814.
[3] Ibid., 1815.

encroachment of death on his life, and the assured persistence of his life beyond death. In life, Hikmet was a beloved poet and dissident hero both in Turkey and among an international Leftist community; he was wrongfully imprisoned from 1938 to 1950 on charges that he had attempted to incite the navy to revolution with his communist poetry, and subsequently exiled from 1951 until the end of his life. In death, he became a potent symbolic figure for the Turkish Left and an enduring point of conflict amidst an ever-changing cultural and political landscape. Hikmet is famous for his inspirational political poetry, in which he frequently and exuberantly declares his own immortality. Less well-known are the macabre afterlife poems he wrote during his lengthy prison sentence when, subjected to a litany of inhumane conditions, Hikmet often depicted his incarceration as a form of death, and himself as an animate corpse. Looking at these darker and largely ignored poems, we see that they in fact necessitate the eternal life postulated in his later and more popular poems, and lay the groundwork for the poet's remarkable afterlife.

A Remarkable (After)Life
I first became aware of the power of Hikmet's enduring memory in Turkish public life during the Gezi Park protests of the summer of 2013. Hikmet's "Invitation" was used repeatedly as a rallying cry during the Gezi Park demonstrations, its final stanza chanted in public squares and written on placards[4]:

> *To live like a tree, solitary and free*
> *and like a forest, as brothers,*
> *this longing is ours.*

Through persistent references to Hikmet's poem, the protesters drew a throughline between the poet's death on June 3, 1963, and the occupation of Gezi Park exactly fifty years later. The poem's final stanza was uniquely fitting for the occasion, blending the natural imagery of the threatened Istanbul park with the larger democratic vision of its occupiers. This same vision – one of a future community joined together by democratic and humanistic ideals – imbues his expansive body of work with a hopeful longing, and continues to make his poetry relevant for diverse political and

---

[4] "Davet" (Invitation) is a part of Hikmet's larger poem *Kuvayi Milliye* (Epic of the War of Independence). Hikmet, *Bütün Şiirleri*, 612.

social movements today both in his native Turkey and around the world.

Struck by the resonance of Hikmet's poem at Gezi Park, I went on to write my doctoral dissertation on Hikmet's afterlife in literature and politics. Entitled *A Shared Longing*, the dissertation identifies a constellation of references to Hikmet's poetry in both his native Turkey and in Turkish communities in Germany. The project also explores what these widespread allusions to Hikmet's poetry and biography can tell us about the way communities are both represented in and created by shared texts. Once I began looking for contemporary references to Hikmet, I found them everywhere: his words are carved into a memorial by a subway station in a busy Berlin square; sung in loose translation by the American folk singer Paul Robeson; printed in the death notices of victims of anti-Leftist violence leading up to the 1980 coup d'état in Turkey; and scattered among the pages of postmodern novels and books of poetry. My research took me to archives in Turkey, Germany, the Netherlands, and the United States, and yielded a trove of documents and ephemera through which Hikmet's memory was not only commemorated but also continuously refashioned. The gathering that occasions this essay, the Nâzım Hikmet Poetry Festival, also represents a rich chapter in Hikmet's afterlife in the United States.

Spending so much time with Hikmet over the past five years, I have often marveled at his staying power. On the one hand, it is no wonder that the man that novelist Orhan Pamuk called the "most extreme exemplar" of Turkey's "great and guilty writers" should remain significant today.[5] The injustices that marked Hikmet's life serve as pressing reminders that our greatest minds and freest thinkers are often the targets of the most vicious abuse in authoritarian contexts. Moreover, given Hikmet's tremendous talent and particular importance for Turkish literary modernity, his continued popularity seems predictable. Yet, on the other hand, it is not a foregone conclusion that lives like Hikmet's will continue to be so fervently admired, and there are myriad talents that fall by the wayside or lose favor over the years. Instead, there is a

---

[5] Orhan Pamuk, "Doya Doya Tükürsünler," *Radikal*, 7. January, 2007 (accessed December 2014); available from:
http://www.radikal.com.tr/kultur/doya-doya-yuzune-tukursunler-802377/

compelling case to be made that Hikmet's powerful legacy is due, at least in part, to his own active participation in authoring his afterlife.

Imprisonment and Virtual Death
In many ways, Hikmet's afterlife began while he was still alive. By the time Hikmet died of a heart attack at the age of sixty-one, he had either been incarcerated or living in exile for nearly half of his life. This meant that, save for the brief period from 1950-51 between his release from prison and his escape to the Soviet Union, Hikmet was removed from Turkish public life beginning with his 1938 arrest. He never saw the Turkish publication of the majority of his written works (among them his most famous work, the epic novel in verse *Human Landscapes from my Country*), as he was a banned author for the entirety of his incarceration and exile. Throughout his life, Hikmet often contemplated and wrote about his death, due in no small part to the torture and inhumane conditions he endured during his trial and sentencing. At several moments, Hikmet believed his death was imminent. He makes this fear explicit in a poem he wrote to his wife Piraye while serving a briefer stint in prison from the spring of 1933 to the summer of 1934[6]:

> *Death*
> *a corpse swinging at the end of a rope.*
> *My heart*
>   *can't accept such a death.*
> *But*
> *you can be sure of it, my love –*
> *if some poor gypsy's*
>   *hairy, black, spider-like hand*
>   *slips a rope*
>   *around my neck,*
> *they will look for fear in Nâzım's blue eyes*
>   *in vain!*

With its stark imagery of the eerie machinery of death, "Letter to my Wife" stands in contrast to the poems he would write during his subsequent prolonged period of imprisonment. These later poems are less concerned with the possibility of immanent physical death than with the death-like experience of imprisonment. Reacting to his original twenty-eight-year sentence doled out by a

---
[6] Hikmet, *Bütün Şiirleri*, 420.

military court in 1938, Hikmet writes to Piraye that he now understands that the court's intention all along was to "'see [him] buried alive,'" and he imagines that he will return home "'crippled and brain-dead.'"[7] As is evident in both his correspondence materials and the myriad death-themed poems he wrote from prison, Hikmet viewed the social and psychological effects of his incarceration as something akin to death.

Hikmet is not alone in thinking of the condition of imprisonment as a virtual or "social" death. Literary scholar Caleb Smith points to the connection between unnerving and inhuman representations of prisoners in literature, and the development of the modern American prison system, which with its "legal, material, and symbolic violence of the penitentiary regime... worked to turn the convict into a kind of animate corpse."[8] Writing about the effects of incarceration on the human psyche, sociologist Joshua Price describes three conditions of imprisonment that make the experience a form of social death: systemic violence, degrading and humiliating treatment, and alienation from familial relations.[9] It must be quickly acknowledged that the conditions in the prisons where Hikmet was held were far different from those of contemporary American penitentiaries, and Hikmet enjoyed periods of intellectual productivity and community life. Moreover, the stigma Hikmet faced as a political prisoner is clearly distinct from that of most individuals incarcerated in the United States. However, he endured and witnessed torture, underwent periods of forced isolation, and experienced continuous emotional and psychological pain due to his separation from his family. In many poems from this period, Hikmet imagines his own place in the world somewhere between life and death.

We see this most clearly in a lesser known verse from 1947, entitled "*Bir ölünüz var*," translated literally as "you have a corpse," or "you have a dead person," and rendered here more idiomatically as "a dead man lives with you." The speaker, who is never identified as

---

[7] As quoted in Saime Göksu and Edward Timms, *Romantic Communist: The Life and Work of Nâzım Hikmet*, (New York: St. Martin's Press, 1999): 147.
[8] Caleb Smith, "Detention without Subjects: Prisons and the Poetics of Living Death," *Texas Studies in Literature and Language* 50.3 (Fall 2008): 224.
[9] Joshua Price, *Prison and Social Death* (New Brunswick: Rutgers University Press, 2015): 5.

a prisoner, describes "the dead" as a ghostly presence in his family home; he "roam[s] the house at night" for months before eventually receding into the background, later reappearing only at the most terrible moments of loneliness. The addressee of the poem is the speaker's beloved, the one accustomed to sharing a bed with "the dead." The beloved is moving on, allowing the intensity of the pain of loneliness to die down; "the sorrow wore off / together with the worn-out sheets." She keeps photographs of "the dead," but looks at them without truly seeing him. For the first three stanzas, the poem can be read literally, giving the reader no reason to think that "the dead" might in fact be a metaphorical construction, a macabre proxy for a living person. The ambiguity enters into the poem in the final two stanzas[10]:

> *A dead man lives with you.*
> *In the dusk like all dead men.*
> *In the dusk one layer closer*
>   *but indistinctly distinguished.*
>
> *A dead man lives with you,*
> *he lies in a tomb,*
> *his flesh hasn't rotted,*
> *his hands and feet quiver.*

In the penultimate stanza, the "dead man" is not simply a "dead man," but rather "*like* all dead men," the added preposition opening up interpretive space between the titular "dead man" and the concept of death itself. The couplet that follows expands this space further, the "dead man" closer to the living than the others ("all dead men"), though hardly distinguishable from them. In the final stanza, the repeated first line, "A dead man lives with you," lends itself to a gruesome reinterpretation; the "dead man" quivers, a living, breathing soul, his flesh still intact, lying trapped in his carceral tomb.

"A dead man lives with you" might be read as a figurative rewriting of a 1943 poem by Hikmet entitled "Ayşe's Letters," which is thought to be a poetic reworking of letters sent by Piraye to Nâzım during the early years of his incarceration. In the poem, a young woman writes forty-eight poem-letters to her husband

---

[10] Hikmet, *Bütün Şiirleri*, 885.

Halil, who is serving a lengthy prison sentence. Each letter tenderly details the events of her domestic life with the couple's young daughter, Leylâ. The letters open a window to a world from which the incarcerated man is absent, a home life filled with gaps where Ayşe's husband ought to be. One letter begins, "I'm writing this letter lying in bed, sick / If you were here, how well you'd take care of me." [11] The two hypothetical clauses in the second line emphasize the missing husband, and an exchange Ayşe recounts a few lines later likewise highlights the missing father[12]:

> I'm writing a message to Dad, Leylâ,' I said
> 'Dad? Who's Dad?' she said
> yawning

The poem only includes Ayşe's letters; Halil's half of the exchange is missing, their contents seen only partially and infrequently through Ayşe's references to his correspondance. Though the letters themselves contain few details of Halil's life, they place the reader in his position, recreating his experience of reading his wife's letters and imagining his own absense. One can imagine "You have a dead man" as Halil's view of the world represented in Ayşe's letters – one in which his painful and prominent absence transforms into a ghostly, and even dreadful presence.

Afterlife and National Memory

Though Hikmet's darker verses about his incarceration are not often referenced by the politicians and protesters who quote the poet today, they help us to understand the perspective from which he wrote his more popular inspirational and directly political poems with themes like immortality and eternal life. Prominent among these is "On the Fifth Day of the Hunger Strike," which Hikmet wrote in 1950 as his hunger strike was drawing international attention and support. The poem is a rallying cry through which Hikmet fashions himself not as a victim but as a heroic idealist. The poem describes his deathly, rapturous state and sets forth a vision for a democratic community free of national

---

[11] "Ayşe's Letters" would later become part of the aforementioned modern epic *Human Landscapes from my Country*. Hikmet, *Bütün Şiirleri*, 831.
[12] Ibid.

borders, which he connects to his supporters' enduring memories of him[13]:

My brothers,
I have no intention of dying.
My brothers,
I know,
  If I do depart this world, I know I will keep living in your minds.

The transformation in this poem from a man close to death to an immortalized Leftist hero is indicative of a close relationship between these two roles Hikmet fashions for himself in his poetry. The heroic afterlife is a necessary antidote to Hikmet's premature social death; the passage from the "animate corpse" to the immortal idealist not only rehabilitates the poet himself, but redeems the nation that brought about his social death in the first place.

Today, Hikmet's afterlife continues to captivate national attention and tether itself to the Turkish Republic's democratic ideal. We can see this nowhere more clearly than in the enduring public debate over the poet's remains. In "Testament," which Hikmet wrote from his exile in Moscow in 1953, the poet famously asks to be buried[14],

In a village graveyard in Anatolia
And if it's not too much trouble
A plane tree could be at my head

The poem continues to inspire high profile pilgrimages to Hikmet's Moscow grave today; these pilgrims bring Anatolian soil to spread on his Moscow grave, or else take handfuls of earth from the grave itself to return to his homeland. An active campaign to return his body to Turkey, begun by the Turkish Writers Union on the poet's seventy-fifth birthday in 1977, regularly resurfaces in the Turkish press at moments of heightened political tension such as the Gezi Park protests of 2013. Like Hikmet's other afterlife poems, "Testament" ties Hikmet's legacy to the future of the Turkish nation; many believe that his resting place will depend on the self-understanding and shared ideals that the national community espouses.

---

[13] Hikmet, *Bütün Şiirleri*, 944.
[14] Hikmet, *Bütün Şiirleri*, 1517.

By linking Hikmet's later, inspirational poems to the earlier, macabre ones, we see how the poet's virtual death through incarceration ultimately generates the need for the cultural narrative of his eternal life. His active and enduring legacy in Turkish political life is a form of national redemption for his premature social death during his lifetime. In this enduring afterlife narrative, the poet comes to stand in for all other incarcerated writers and freethinkers in the Turkish Republic, his abiding presence a reminder of their absence from public life. Hikmet, the originator of this shared cultural narrative, continues to hold sway today, ensuring that his legacy has a necessary role to play in the national community's negotiation of democratic ideals.

Works Cited

1. Hikmet Ran, Nazim. *Bütün Şiirleri*. Istanbul: Yapı Kredi Yayınları, 2011.
2. Pamuk, Orhan. "Doya Doya Tükürsünler." *Radikal*. 7. January, 2007. Web. December 2014.
3. Price, Joshua. *Prison and Social Death*. New Brunswick: Rutgers University Press, 2015.
4. Smith, Caleb. "Detention without Subjects: Prisons and the Poetics of Living Death." *Texas Studies in Literature and Language* 50.3 (Fall 2008).

Jill Stockwell is a postdoctoral research associate at the Princeton University Center for Human Values working on Turkish and Turkish-German cultural and literary studies. Her interests include leftist intellectual history, intertextuality, postmodernism, and migration. Her current research focuses on the mid-century literary left in Turkey, and the centrality of transnational affiliations in the development of literary postmodernism(s). Stockwell holds a Ph.D. in Comparative Literature from Princeton University, and is a Fulbright and Social Science Research Council scholar. She is also affiliated with the Prison Teaching Initiative as a research associate.

Nazim Hikmet: Harbinger of Hope

Greg Dawes

For Debbie McKenzie

The mark of a great poet is his or her ability to reach out to a broad readership and to encompass myriad concerns, passions, tragedies, joys, commitments, and reflections about life and to communicate those themes in remarkably innovative workings and reworkings of poetic language. In my view, Nazim Hikmet's verse, written over a forty-year period in his native Turkish and translated into more than fifty languages, does exactly that. There are readers here who have the good fortune of reading Hikmet's poetry in the original Turkish and understand the nuances of the culture and his place in it in a way that readers of his works in translation cannot hope to grasp. There are others who read his poems impeded and yet very inspired by cultural translations. There are those who praise Hikmet as a proto-modernist who created a revolution in Turkish poetry by employing free verse, typographical distribution of words, thematic juxtaposition, colloquial speech, and an autobiographical mode. Still others are drawn to him for his collage-like, intimate portrayals of the Turkish countryside and its bustling cities and the love poems that emanated from those sites.[15] Still others find in Hikmet's work that rare combination of personal confessions and left-wing socio-political convictions. His work is clearly all that and more, and that is why we keep returning to it in search of the expected and unexpected. One could reiterate what the Mexican poet José Emilio Pacheco said of Hikmet's good friend Pablo Neruda: "he is reborn every day because there is always someone who is reading him for the first time and someone else

---

[15] Talat Sait Halman, "Nazim Hikmet: Turkey's Romantic Revolutionary" in Ruth Christie, Richard McKane, Talat Sait Halman Trans., *Nazim Hikmet: Beyond the Walls, Selected Poems* (London: Anvil Press Poetry, 2002): 11.

who is re-reading him with new eyes. Not to do so would impoverish our lives."[16]

Due to the autobiographical mode in his poetry it is almost impossible to separate his vocation as a versemaker from his passionate commitments, both personal and political. Hikmet spent thirteen years of his life in jail and thirteen years in exile because of his militancy in the Communist Party and his work for Turkey's national liberation. Almost half of his life was spent behind bars or in lands that weren't his. Granted, sometimes he sought out exile, as when, in 1921, already a celebrity poet in his native Turkey, he went to the Soviet Union to learn about the revolution and to study at the University of Workers of the East in Moscow. There, in the USSR, Futurism held sway and Hikmet's method was clearly impacted by its influence.[17] Using alliteration, assonance, onomatopoeia, and typographical displacement, he began writing in free verse about concrete topics, and, in so doing, revolutionized modern Turkish poetry. His discovery of the literary avant-garde, then, went hand in hand with his deepening leftist political commitments. Changes in form accompanied transformations in content.

To convey his political and individual ideas more readily and in a pioneering way, by the 1930s he had developed a "dynamic synthesis," which aimed at transcending the one-dimensional "active realism" he had developed in the 1920s.[18] His best work, it could be argued, was published after that discovery. Besides his masterpiece, "The Epic of Sheikh Bedreddin," penned in 1936, I am thinking particularly of his "Poems Written between 9 and 10 at Night" during World War II. I mention this short work because it encapsulates the powerful and tragic tension between love poems written to his wife Pirayé and his own incarceration, and thus underlines the strained unity between the personal and the political. Readers of all types are drawn into Hikmet's world in this context. Though we know his radical political activity landed him jail and thus can't be surprised that he is there, we can't but feel

---

[16] José Emilio Pacheco, "Prólogo: Para llegar a Isla Negra" in Pablo Neruda's *Memorial de Isla Negra* (Buenos Aires: Random House/Mondadori, 2004): 8. My translation.
[17] Talat Sait Halman, 10.
[18] Ibid., 14.

empathy or compassion for the man in confinement who wrestles with his solitude, separation from his dear wife, distance from nature, and the remoteness from the political events he helped shape. "They've taken us prisoner, / They've locked us up," he says in a poem composed on September 26th, 1945:

> *me inside the walls,*
> *you outside.*
> *But that's nothing.*
> *The worst*
> *Is when people – knowingly or not –*
> *carry prison inside themselves...*
> *Most people have been forced to do this,*
> *honest, hard-working, good people,*
> *who deserve to be loved as much as I love you...*[19]

That point is also outlined in a poignant way in "It's this Way," published in 1948:

> *I stand in the advancing light,*
> *My hands hungry, the world beautiful.*
> *My eyes can't get enough of the trees –*
> *They're so hopeful, so green.*
> *A sunny road runs through the mulberries,*
> *I'm at the window of the prison infirmary.*
> *I can't smell the medicines –*
> *Carnations must be blooming nearby.*
> *It's this way:*
> *Being captured is beside the point,*
> *The point is not to surrender.*[20]

As readers we follow the speaker's re-discovery of a seemingly limitless nature until we are confronted with the jolting reference to his limitations, to the "prison infirmary." In the next to the last stanza, we revisit that juxtaposition in a compressed manner: the carnations' boundlessness and vitality contrasts sharply with the sense of confinement embodied in the medicines. And that antithesis, restated in the last lines, underlines the speaker's

---

[19] Randy Blasing and Mutlu Konuk Trans., *Poems of Nazim Hikmet* (New York: Persea Books, 2002): 101.
[20] Ibid., 135.

determination and the power of his political beliefs, which are fused with nature's ostensibly inexhaustible and radiant beauty. Poems like these, once we internalized them, make us want to re-read and to continue reading Hikmet's verse. We come to his verse looking for tragic strength, for errors, for altruism and we find them throughout his work.

I found out about Nazim Hikmet some ten years ago thanks to Pablo Neruda's poetry and memoirs. Fortunately, a year later I was able to teach a world literature course on the poetry of Bertolt Brecht, Federico García Lorca, Muriel Rukeyser, Pablo Neruda and Nazim Hikmet. Though there were some students who were taken by each of these poets, the majority gravitated toward Hikmet. After what was one of the most intensely satisfying courses I've taught in my twenty years at North Carolina State University, I would inevitably run into students on campus who would want to continue the discussion, especially about Hikmet's poetry. And just this past fall, I received a long e-mail from one of the students, now teaching English in Japan, who said that Hikmet had changed his life and that he kept re-reading his poems to give him guidance and hope. And last year also, before the onset of our friend's cancer, I read Hikmet's wonderful poem "I Want to Die Before You" to our friend Debbie and her husband Mac. At Debbie's funeral Mac asked me to read an edited version of that poem. In closing, I would like to read it again in honor of Debbie and the great poet Nazim Hikmet.

"I want to Die Before You"

I
Want to die before you.
Do you think the one coming after
Will find the one gone before?
I don't think so.
Best to cremate me
And put me in a jar
      Over the stove in your room.
Let the jar be a glass one,
Of transparent, white glass,
      So that you can see me...

You understand my faithfulness:
I've given up the earth,
I've given up being a flower
> *To stay by your side.*

I am become dust,
I am living by your side.
Then, when you die,
You'll come into my jar.
There we'll live together,
Your ashes in my ashes,
Until a careless bride,
Or a disloyal grandchild
Throws us out from there.
But we
Will mingle
Together so
Till then
That our particles when thrown out in the rubbish
Will fall side by side.
We'll go deep together into the earth.
And if one day a wild flower
From this dampened earth shoots forth
There will definitely
Be two flowers on its stem
> *One you,*
> *One me.*[21]

---

[21] *Nazim Hikmet: Beyond the Walls, Selected Poems*, 153-54.

Greg Dawes is a distinguished professor of Latin American Studies and Cultural Theory at North Carolina State University and editor of the peer reviewed electronic journal, *A Contracorriente* and the press Editorial A Contracorriente. He is from the United States but spent seven years of his childhood in Argentina and has spent time in several other Latin American countries as well, particularly Chile. His books include *Aesthetics and Revolution: Nicaraguan Poetry, 1979-1990*, *Verses Against the Darkness: Pablo Neruda's Poetry and Politics*, *Poetas Ante La Modernidad: Las Ideas Esteticas y Politicas de Vallejo, Huidobro, Neruda y Paz* and *Multiforme y comprometido: Pablo Neruda después de 1956*. He is currently working on a book on Whitman and Neruda.

Nâzım Hikmet and The Poetics of Confinement

Erdağ Göknar

Outside and inside are both intimate – they are always ready to be reversed, to exchange their hostility. If there exists a border-line surface between such an inside and outside, this surface is painful on both sides.... In this drama of intimate geometry, where should one live?
– Gaston Bachelard, The Poetics of Space

I. Inside/Outside

Among other things, Nâzım Hikmet's poetry demonstrates engagement with two dominant conceptual spaces. Broadly speaking, these might be described as "inside" (*içeride*) and "outside" (*dışarıda*). Obviously, these are the spaces of incarceration. However, this is only the most literal manifestation. These spaces are also metaphorical and representative of other discourses based on binary thought. That is, such a poetic structure conjures the bases of disciplinary (in both senses of the word) thought systems: self and other (psychology), the private and the public (sociology), or the individual and the collective (history). These disciplines relate to themes in Hikmet's work, themes of identity, nation-state, and autobiography. In aesthetic terms, his work plays with the related notions of inclusion and exclusion, which might reflect, for example, the longing of separation between lover and beloved – a common leitmotif in Ottoman and Sufi literature. His use of poetic space allows modes of the lyrical and narrative to reflect representations of self and history. The meeting of inside and outside produces a "painful surface," a border of affect, that results in the imagination of resistance or (re)union. Ideologically, it might represent the juxtaposition between nationalist and socialist worldviews. These tropes allow for a number of interpretations of what constitutes poetic space and what–in the "drama of intimate geography"–is constituted by it: whether aesthetic object or sentient subject.

Despite this multitude of perspectives, Hikmet's work is often limited to two dominant readings based on dissidence and humanism, which mark a confinement in his reception. Within the national tradition, the dominant reading of his work is one of secular humanism. On the outside, in a world of limited translations, it is based on dissidence. This piece, in three sections, will defer to other types of readings, ones that reflect Hikmet's poetics rather than his (inter)national representations.

Once inside and outside are established, Hikmet's poetic gesture transgresses and subverts the divisions between them. At times this is accomplished through an emotion, memory, expectation or an ideal. The following short excerpt from "Letters from a Man in Solitary" demonstrates this point:

> *It's five o'clock, dear.*
>   *Outside,*
>   *with its dryness,*
>   *eerie whispers,*
>
>   *mud roof,*
> *and lame, skinny horse*
>   *standing motionless in infinity*
> *- I mean, it's enough to drive a man inside mad with sorrow -*
> *outside, with all its machinery and all its art,*
> *a steppe night alights red onto treeless space.*

The division of space is quite apparent, with the inside delineated as the realm of perception and affect, while the outside is infinite and abstract. The two spaces are united by the order and synchronicity of time: 5 pm, the end of the day. However, there is movement between them. The gesture of this passage reveals that the poetic act is one of crossing and transgression between realms. More importantly, the poem itself encompasses both inside and outside and includes the reader in a locus of belonging and witness that is neither one nor the other. This new third space is one of intimacy.

The image of the last line plays with another spatial metaphor, that of absence and presence: The description of the night, a circadian phase, alighting onto the absence, rather than the presence, of trees. Suddenly, the reader perceives imagery through the negative space of absent objects. The absence of a bird (freedom) or the tree (a motif of grounding and belonging that reappears in Hikmet's work, notably "The Walnut Tree") is compensated for by the expectation of landing/perching by redness. This is the all-encompassing color of sunset as well as a symbol of the socialist ideal. The consciousness of the inside (incarceration) is matched with the natural cycle of days that describes freedom in spatial and ideological terms. This is emphasized by an absent bird coming to rest in an absent tree. The following meaning is reinforced: No freedom and no home except in the imagination, in yearning and in the intimacy of poetic space. (In this drama, the binary of inside/outside is conflated with that of longing/belonging.)

Yet, this space is one that permits inversion. We might come to realize, reading the work of the poet, that the confined speaker is actually on the *outside* of a socialist discourse of inclusion and the *inside* of a nationalist discourse of exclusion. The realms approach a relative status such that one does not exist without the other, they are dependent and assume relational permanence. That is to say, "treeless space" is neither inside nor outside.

A similar intimacy, through the imagery of expanding interiority can be seen in "Istanbul Detention Center." Here, Hikmet emphasizes how the "I" of the voice expands to encompass various exteriorities, various degrees of division and separation, that gather into a collective. The outside limit is "you" evoking the lover/beloved metaphor:

> *The Istanbul Detention Center yard*
> *sunlit winter day after rain,*
> *as clouds, red terra cotta, walls, and my face*
>   *tremble from puddles on the ground -*
> *I, bearing everything brave and base,*
> *everything strong and frail in my self, I -*
> *the world, my country, I think of you...*

The speaker's visage, a symbol of identity, is reflected in rippled water – ephemeral and transitory – as part of a pastiche that includes "walls" of confinement. Between the "I" and "you", rests the painful impediment of all other things, including my country (*memleket*) and the world. Here, the pastiche of nature, walls, and the face alludes to a fragmentation that re-appears in Hikmet's work and is contrasted to (re)union. The exteriors and fragments are being reduced through an expanding interior poetic space. What is highlighted is the limit of the "detained" as described by humanistic qualities and adjectives. Rather it is the *thought* of "you", an intimate object of desire, which repeats the gesture of transcendence of the self (a movement outside, toward the metaphysical), contact with another, and the transgression of the border between inside and outside. The "you" here thus becomes any exteriority. The poem indicates that Hikmet's poetics is predicated on establishing the relativity of barriers of detention and incarceration. In addition to the prison wall is the space of separation between individuals. In a humanist vein, this condition does not prevent expression or communication of desire. On the contrary, it becomes the basis for a poetics of movement from longing toward belonging.

The same condition of inclusion/exclusion and connection is represented allegorically in the following painting by Hikmet:

Centered in the image is a clock that marks a time of synchronicity between inside and outside (as in the "Solitary" fragment above). The figures embody a state of yearning and longing, something that describes a desire for movement out of the interior space of disciplined bodies. The fact that they are half-naked reveals a variety of discipline anticipating examination and the force of institutional regularity. Furthermore, the forms are deprived of individuality. The door labeled "doctor" is one of potential that might possibly transform their condition of affliction. In other words, what is being awaited is an encounter with someone from the "outside". Healing emerges from this encounter. The expectation alone is unifying and inclusive. Here, returning to an economy of desire, "lover" manifests as a patient and the "beloved" as a doctor. This painting is both specific to a particular context and a metaphor for spatial and poetic structure and organization. Yet, it also allows for political commentary: an educated, elite individual (whether doctor or artist) is counterposed to a representation of the masses. There is a modernist indictment in the painting that corresponds to the responsibility of the intelligentsia toward the people. The indistinct faces directed toward the viewer underscore this message of responsibility. The viewer, as a witness to this space, also holds the possibility for its transformation. We have been allowed access to the inside, yet we remain outside, in a liminal state of exception.

II. Narrative Incarceration

Nâzım Hikmet's use of free verse negotiates between lyrical and narrative modes of expression. The poetics of inside-outside become even more relevant in Hikmet's longer epics. His magnum opus, *Human Landscapes from My Country* (*memleket*), is a cinematic novel in free verse made up of vignettes depicting an array of individuals and social relations through the plot of a train journey from Istanbul into Anatolia. Here, Hikmet's focus moves from the dispossessed to the wealthy, from prostitutes, and criminals to industrialists and bankers. Written between 1939 and 1950, the work is semi-autobiographical and contains historical descriptions of WWI, the Turkish "War of Independence", and WWII. The epic work of socialist literature follows the main autobiographical character, a political prisoner named Hilmi who is being transported to another prison. Anatolia appears in this work through vignettes that describe around 300 different people. The verse-novel is also important, not least of all, because it addresses a recurring theme both internally within Turkish letters and from an outsider perspective: the "incarceration narrative". This narrative also establishes spaces of interiority and exteriority.

The types of "incarceration" encountered in *Human Landscapes* move from the literal to the metaphorical. Hikmet wrote a majority of *Human Landscapes* during prison terms amounting to twelve years: a work of testimony from the incarcerated intellectual. Embedded in the longer socialist poem are references and extensive quotes from a shorter nationalist epic of Hikmet's called *Kuvâyi Millye (National Resistance)*, written about the local insurgencies and "war of independence" against the Allied occupations after WWI and the comprador Ottoman government. This valorization of the struggle for "national self-determination" is a long free-verse narrative of about 80 pages that mingles historical events, official national history, and poetic vignettes describing the heroism of villagers-cum-soldiers who represent the efforts of "common men and women" in bringing about an "anti-imperial and anti-colonial" victory.

National Resistance was written while Hikmet was in three different prisons between 1939-41. Earlier sections were even published as intermezzos along with the 1938 edition of Mustafa Kemal's famous six-day *Speech*. However, Hikmet also later includes sections of this shorter epic into *Human Landscapes*, but embeds it in another drama. Kitchen staffers in the dinner car are reading the poem to each other, between shifts. Whereas the first version ends with national victory as a villager/soldier looks out over the Mediterranean from Izmir in 1922, the second ends with the death of a villager on the battlefield of the "war of independence" and then brings us back to the train and the context of WWII. The "war of independence", in this second version, is open-ended, without real conclusion; the battle against anti-imperialism and fascism continues undecided. By juxtaposing nationalist and socialist epics, Hikmet allows us to re-read distinct ideological and historical discourses together, thus transforming the Turkist account into a more encompassing one of social critique. Conflated in these scenes are the transport of prisoners, the high-speed journey through Anatolia in the confines of a train wagon, the recitation of the national epic, the conditions of labor, and the promise of social liberation. In short, confinements and narratives, which are actually describing confinements *in* narrative, paramount among them, the national master narrative. Here, the inside-outside trope re-emerges in the scope of ideology such that Hikmet's poetic space is inclusive of both.

Suddenly, another story emerges, one that links the on-going conditions of an emerging Third World country to other related contexts of socialist struggle. The inversion Hikmet brings about by first seeing the national epic from the inside as self-determination, and secondly, seeing it from the outside as a mechanism of sacrifice and exploitation, allows the reader to access two divergent points-of-view, to pass through "walls", to escape as it were. If there is a didactic function in Hikmet's work, it rests in attaining the consciousness of another vantage or point-of-view on *memleket* (the land, context, and people of one's birth and familiarity) as opposed to the more abstract nation (*vatan*). Thus, the prison narrative here describes resistance to the imposition of ungrounded identities through discourses backed by sovereign power. The prison is a shadow space of the cultural revolution, it is where those who do not "convert" in the inquisition of modernity end up.

Hikmet, thus, in a severe way, suffers the contradictory fate of being included and excluded from the national tradition. When he escaped the country for the Soviet Union, he was stripped of his Turkish citizenship – which was only restored early in 2009. He lived in exile, primarily in Moscow, until his death in 1963. A dedicated communist and humanist, over 25 volumes of his work exists in Turkish, only a small fraction has been translated into English. The reason for this, I believe, is that he is only read through discourses of dissidence and humanism. Once that political subtext is articulated, the literature itself becomes secondary.

III. *Memleket*: Belonging

To return to the inside-outside theme, we might conclude at another level, that of *memleket*, a recurring trope in Hikmet's work. Though this is often translated as "country", this fails to capture the nuances of the word in Turkish. *Memleket* for Hikmet is an imagined space of belonging and intimacy; a place of memory and nostalgia where one would like to return to, but cannot. It is inaccessible except in poetic space. *Memleket* is a reunion with place, a place that is neither inside nor outside.

It is evident that Nâzım Hikmet is read through discourses of humanism from the national traditions and through discourses of dissidence in the "West". My contention is that these are limiting approaches to his aesthetic and artistic work. As the above examples should make clear, in addition to these two dominant approaches, he is moreover engaged in establishing a poetics of intimacy. If this reading began with conceptual notions of the experience of space, it comes to conclusion at the possibility of other types of readings. Hikmet does respond to the question in the epigraph, "Where should one live in the intimate geometry of inside and outside?" He answers by emphasizing the desire to draw exteriority toward the inside of poetic sensibility. This is what establishes intimacy in poetic space. *Memleket*, for Hikmet, does not exist on the outside, but in the poetic space of an interiorized exterior.

Erdağ Göknar is Associate Professor of Asian & Middle Eastern Studies at Duke University and an award-winning literary translator. He holds an MFA in Creative Writing from the University of Oregon and a Ph.D. in Middle East Studies from the University of Washington. He has published various articles on Turkish literary culture as well as three novel translations (most recent editions listed): Nobel laureate Orhan Pamuk's *My Name is Red* (Everyman's Library 2010); Atiq Rahimi's *Earth and Ashes* (from Dari, Other Press 2010); and A.H. Tanpınar's *A Mind at Peace* (Archipelago 2011). He is the co-editor of *Mediterranean Passages: Readings from Dido to Derrida* (UNC Press 2008) and the author of the academic study, *Orhan Pamuk, Secularism and Blasphemy: The Politics of the Turkish Novel* (Routledge 2013). His current book project, *Occupied Istanbul: Turkish Subject-Formation from Trauma to Trope*, examines the cultural legacy of the Allied occupation of Istanbul between 1918-23. His most recent book is a collection of poetry, *Nomadologies* (Turtle Point, 2017).

Nazim Hikmet: The Forms of Exile

Mutlu Konuk Blasing

Nazim began his life as a poet with a decisive break from the traditional meters of Turkish poetry. Free verse in Turkish had no precedent in the 19th-century; it was Nazim's invention. Two distinct meters had ruled Turkish poetry for centuries. Syllabics, at one time called "finger measures" because of the counting involved, was the form of Turkish oral folk poetry, a meter suited to the sonic shape of Turkish. In syllabic verse, all the lines have the same number of syllables, and each line is divided into segments with "stops," which cannot come mid-word, between them. Because the line forms had given patterns that determined where the pauses came, the poet worked under the extreme constraints of the rhythmic system. Word breaks or phrase breaks had to come at given places, and lexical and syntactic units had to adjust themselves to the pre-determined metrical patterns.

Aruz, on the other hand, was the quantitative meter of Ottoman court poetry. Derived from Arabic measures, the meter was based on the length of syllables. There were eighteen "feet" or arrangements of long and short syllables, ranging from feet of one long syllable to feet of five-syllable combinations of long and short syllables, and twenty-four "molds" of these feet made for the range of the possible rhythms of lines. Ottoman court poetry was written verse, with a syntax and a vocabulary heavily influenced by Arabic and Persian. Arabic script was "peculiarly inappropriate," in Bernard Lewis's apt term, for Turkish, which is a vowel-rich language, and the script encouraged the influx of Arabic and Persian words into Turkish. Similarly, *aruz* meters favored borrowings in vocabulary, especially from Persian, because the meter did not fit Turkish. Thus written Ottoman poetry, with its borrowed vocabulary and forms, was in a language inaccessible to the common Turkish speaker. The unsuitability of the alphabet had led to general illiteracy by segregating written and spoken languages. "In Ottoman Turkey," Lewis writes, "an illiterate man could not hope to understand a normal written text even if it were read aloud to him" (436). Writing and speaking were two separate languages.

Nazim said more than once that he did not know Ottoman, and his emergence as a poet coincides with Turkey's change, in 1928, to the Latin alphabet, a much simpler phonetic script that was responsive to the sounds of spoken Turkish. Ataturk's alphabet reform converged with Nazim's drive to close the gap between spoken and written languages in a poetry that would be accessible to any common speaker of Turkish. His understandable aim was to be understood by any speaker of Turkish. A modernist poet as technically daring as any of his generation, Nazim was also in the mainstream of his nation's creation as a modern, democratic republic. Fahri Erdinç recalls teaching adults in village schools, where he would read Nazim to the peasants. One man, his hunting buddy, said after hearing Nazim, "Teacher, what you read can't be a poem—even *I* understand it" (32).

During the years that Nazim was in print in Turkey, there were other means of circulating his work among people who, for example, wouldn't think of buying a book of poetry or, living in remote areas, had no access to one. But Nazim made sure that they could all understand him. He wrote Kemal Tahir that "people should find a response—in the terms of art—to all their questions. I mean, when they're in love and need to read a love poem; I mean, when they're fighting and need to read a fighting poem, when they're defeated and need to read a poem of hope, or when they've triumphed and need to read a poem of joy; I mean, when they're growing old and need to resolve the matter of aging, when they're sick, when they listen to nature, when they want to solve social problems—in short, our people should never put down our books at any moment" (368-69).

Ottoman court poetry and folk poetry had also, in effect, restricted the historical visibility/audibility of experiences that did not fall within the limits of their generic lyric *topoi*—love, loss, time, death, and so on—and the vocabulary that addressed such universal topics in the two traditional meters. The pre-existing forms came with their politics: generic rules and political ideologies reinforced each other to withstand encroachments from "outside" poetic discourse. The two kinds of poetry of two different socioeconomic classes—a privileged class and a dispossessed class at a great remove from the center of Ottoman court power—conspired to protect a poetic domain, if a domain strictly divided within itself.

Nazim broke down those barriers, crossing borders without a passport—which became a habit with him. He did not believe in closing borders between different meters, between poetry and prose ("there is no Great Wall of China," he wrote, "prohibiting passage from one to the other"), or between the different subject matter that the two genres covered, any more than he observed class or national borders. Nazim's free-verse lines varied wildly in length, and his poems, especially the early ones, often took up the whole page, using all the visual resources of typographical design. He delivered his poems in a public, highly rhetorical voice intensified by his use of devices like insistent alliteration, strong rhymes, refrains, and repetitions at irregular intervals. His language was direct, spoken Turkish. With his new forms and diction, it became possible for him to address different kinds of subject matter and bring current social realities into the poetic domain.

All this is by way of background for my topic today: the forms of Nazim's late poetry, written in exile after 1951. He continued to write the free verse that he had introduced and used throughout his work, but he also wrote in two other, very different forms at both extremes of his free-verse norms. Many of his exile poems are composed in syllabic meters or have syllabic passages. Even when they're not quite regular, they have the feel of syllabics, which, with their long oral history, carry the historical weight of "Turkishness." But, while Nazim wrote a number of such measured poems in his exile years, he also has late poems written in an entirely new form for him. These come in very long lines that sometimes branch off into prose, but they are not prosy because of their breathless pace and exhilarating speed that is not without its component of dread. His syllabic poems—with their constraints of syllable counts, predictable rhyme schemes, and refrains—radically contrast with the expansiveness of poems where lines regularly overflow into small blocks of prose in print. Such verse is impelled by rhythmic phrasing alone; it is not measured, but the rhythmic impulsion driving it communicates great urgency and gives a necessity to its shape, thus fulfilling one function of meter.

This new kind of free-verse poetry comes with no punctuation, foregoing one traditional way of orienting the reader of a printed text. By contrast, while folk poems in oral forms are normally printed without punctuation, Nazim's syllabic poems are usually punctuated, but his poems in free-flow lines are not. In a letter from Bursa Prison, he stated a rule: poetic syntax that depends on commas, semicolons, and periods indicates a weak word order. A poem should be clear without the directives of punctuation and should rely on syntactic drive alone; his poems with the extra long lines work on this principle. Although they have the look of Whitmanic overflow lines, they are essentially different, because Whitman's long lines depend on end punctuation.

These two forms of exile poetry reflect Nazim's dominant themes between 1951 and 1963, the year of his death. Formally and thematically, they pull us in different directions. During his exile, Nazim lived in Moscow but traveled widely as a member of the administrative board of the World Peace Council. After thirteen years of confinement in prison, he was constantly on the move during his exile, his travels spanning not only Europe but extending to the Asian Turkic republics, China, Egypt, Cuba, and Tanganyika; in his words, "I traveled through Europe, Asia, and Africa with my dream / only the Americans didn't give me a visa." But another constant in these years of frenzied travel was his yearning for his wife and son back in Turkey, his city, his land, its landscapes and seascapes—a yearning he expressed in some of his most moving poems. In his late verse, Nazim was negotiating his exile experience, at once returning to forms rooted in the Turkish language and landscapes and registering the unprecedented conditions of his deracination, homelessness, and travel through global spaces.

How can we engage these two forms in some kind of dialogue? In his exile poems, Nazim's longing for the earth of his homeland is painfully clear: Istanbul and its seas are his emotional dwellings, and he compulsively returns to what he cannot forget:

> *the poet Nicholas Guillen went back to Havana long ago*
> *for years we sat in the hotel lobbies of Europe and Asia*
>   *drinking the loss of our cities drop by drop*
> *two things are forgotten only with death*
> *the face of our mothers and the face of our cities*
>
>   (PNH 244)

Unlike his syllabic poems, Nazim's late, free-flowing poems are consciously rooted in groundlessness—in the sense of the ground being pulled out from under the poet. The exile's persisting question is "Who am I?"; Nazim's two forms give two different answers to that question.

In Nazim's case, the precariousness of the present in his exploding temporal and spatial world may also be understood in terms of the tension between nationalist, internationalist, and global models of modernism. While folk forms often voiced the wanderings of displaced, troubadour poets, their forms, for Nazim and his Turkish readers, would carry a sense of "home"—a local, native poetic ground. But his run-on free forms speed through global spaces and times and project a different kind of homelessness, on a different scale.

The troubadour, the *ozan* or *aşik*, is exiled from his "home"; an internal émigré, he wanders widely, but always through recognizable rural landscapes. Folk poems are very much part of the real world, in that they're not abstract, but the folk tradition is also connected to mystical thought predating the Turks' adoption of Islam. The poet is exiled from his "love," both earthly love and a figure of mystical love, the *aşik*'s real "home," which is, in turn, equated with language itself. In one well-known example by the 17th-century *aşik* Karacaoğlan, as the poet's "wild heart wanders outcast," he finds Elif, his beloved, everywhere he looks: the snowflakes "scatter Elif Elif" in the wind, the "Little wildflowers of the plains / Breathe their perfumes Elif Elif," and "The pen she holds in her white hand / Spells the letters Elif Elif." Elif, a girl's name, is also the first letter of the Arabic alphabet and, as such, comes to stand for the one and only Allah. More accurately, Allah and writing stand for each other; in this synecdoche, letters spell the one and only Allah, and Allah is revealed in letters. In other words, in the beginning was the alphabet.

In contrast to his syllabic poems with their historical, literary, and cultural roots, Nazim's poems in overflowing lines are cosmopolitan in their settings, and they speed through vast spaces on trains and planes. "Things I Didn't Know I Loved" takes place on a train; "Straw-Blond," another major poem of his exile years, is signed off with *"Trains Warsaw-Krakow-Prague-Moscow-Paris-Havana-Moscow."* Yet the poem also suggests a search for union with a mystical love, beyond Nazim's actual straw-blond beloved. Certain lines in "Straw-Blond," such as the reference to Rumi "whirling in space," encourage amplification, and the Turkish title, *"Saman Sarısı,"* also suggests cosmic whirling; the Milky Way galaxy in Turkish is named *"Saman Yolu"* or the "The Straw Path." This association of Nazim's beloved and the galaxy is unavoidable in Turkish, and it links his latest reckless love, for Vera, to global travel and his headlong rush to say, "Hello, universe." In fact, both types of exile poems are driven by death—the first by its inevitability (wherever, however, whenever) and the second by its imminence. The free-flow poems have a sense less of fate and endings and more of an expanding universe. From this perspective, Nazim's modern free form allows for a kind of mystical cosmic expansion, rather than a mere submission to the inevitable.

Why would the experience of exile branch out into these two forms? Folk poems, which address the human condition of alienation and exile from God, also represent the lamentations of tribal peoples and their longings for familiar landscapes. Under their surface resignation, however, these poems protest political and economic exclusion from power, for the relationship between the poet-lover and the disdainful beloved also has an edge of hostility. The feeling of loss pervading these poems is not a modern nostalgia for a lost agrarian past synchronized with the rhythms of nature. We're still in a natural setting, but with a regret that "the rose gardens now lie in ruin"—a regret more like a longing. Nazim's use of this form recalls a tradition that puts his personal displacement "on the map" of current history.

The choice of syllabic forms or forms that have a syllabic feel is in itself an elegiac move, as in "In the Snowy Night Woods":

> *The beeches deep in snow,*
> *I walk the dark woods*
> *In sorrow, sorrow.*
> *Your hand, where is your hand?*
>
> *The snow the color of moonlight,*
> *My boots heavy in the night,*
> *The song that's sung in me*
> *Is calling me, but where?*
>
> (PNH 176)

This form, suitable to the subject of a "very sick, very exiled poet," gives a different edge to poems that address current international issues. For example, here is "Once in Japan":

> *In Japan once there was a girl,*
> *a little girl still just a child.*
> *Then a cloud gathered in the sky*
> *whose only business was to kill.*
> *This cloud took the girl's grandmother,*
> *so dear to this poor little girl,*
> *and hurled her ashes through the air.*
> *Then down it swooped again, faster*
> *than before, and snatched her father*
> *and then the little girl herself.*
> *Ever more ravenous each day,*
> *it's on the prowl for new victims.*
> *Atomic death is now its name;*
> *it bellows where it's dark and dim.*
> *Let's join forces all together*
> *and silence this savage monster.*
> *Let's all join on the battlefield*
> *and all together crush this beast.*
>
> 1963
>
> (Trans. Randy Blasing and Mutlu Konuk)

Nazim's syllabics and the folk feel of his narrative strangely counterpoint his call to arms. His summons to the "battlefield" is also an odd rhetorical move in a plea for disarmament, and his

43

diction—with its medieval "savage monster" and "beast"—heightens the tension between the folk form and current global emergencies. This makes for an effective poem, even as the formal sense of fatedness tonally compromises the battle call; the poem acknowledges an unending struggle against "monsters"—not just "once" but over and over. And Nazim's use of syllabics, suitable for musical adaptation, helped circulate the peace message of such poems through other media, including popular songs.

As opposed to his formally grounded poems in syllabics, Nazim's long poems written in exile are poems of displacement and incessant motion, both in physical space and inner landscapes and both in their forms and their explicit themes. In "Havana Report," some lines run on for half a page, as descriptions of external scenes and impressions blend seamlessly, in an associative matrix, with subjective responses of thoughts, feelings, and memories. The repetition of certain words and phrases, Asım Bezirci writes, both provide resting points—like "landings on steps of stairs"—and serve to return us to the main subject (219). The figure of "landings" that he uses to describe the formal movement of returns and repetitions in the text's flow is apt in more than one sense. In his final years, after two heart attacks, Nazim could not climb a flight of stairs without resting on the landings; in their apartment building, Vera Tulyakova tells us, he had a chair placed on each landing.

"Straw-Blond" is Nazim's most ambitious poem in this late mode. Here, the moving site of the train brings together memories, fantasies, feelings, and thoughts; it is a figure of the time that flows constantly yet, at the same time is the "'backbone' that holds up the structure or the 'river bed' that guides the meanderings and straightenings, the slowings down and speedings up, of the river's course to reunite with the sea" — "the great cemetery of rivers," in Nazim's words (Bezirci 224; PNH 252). But just to say that "Straw-Blond" is about time and love would not accurately convey Nazim's "mastery of segues, even as he speaks about his personal life, to social concerns and openings to universal horizons" (Bezirci 225). Nazim's heart condition may suggest a physiological basis for his late, breathless rhythms, but his repetitions and refrains, his landings, also affirm that, as he puts it in "Angina Pectoris," his "heart still beats with the most distant stars" (PNH 136).

Indeed, Nazim's spatial location is split or doubled: he's both on the outside looking into the train and inside the train looking out. In temporal terms, the subject/object is both in the past, gazing at the present, and in the present, gazing at the past. He is the spectator of his times—and his own time—from both termini. The train runs right through the speaker on these parallel tracks, which can only meet in optical illusions. The train here is a figure of the condition of exile—living on the go, in two time zones, and speaking their different languages. Set in an amorphous present, the poem is porous to the past and the future, both on the scale of personal history and on the immediate scale of clock time. It coheres around a theme—"her hair straw-blond eyelashes blue"—and refrains, as time flows backward and forward at once: "time sped on we were nearing midnight"; "time sped on I was nearing midnight"; "time speeds on we're nearing midnight"; "time speeds on midnight approaches"; "time sped backward"; "time speeds on midnight recedes." When time speeds in reverse, it goes all the way back to his "big Istanbul" as it "wakes up from sleep" from "the ashes of a brazier" (PNH 244). When time speeds forward, it is rushing forward to death and dissolution in the "universe."

In such a high-speed poem, without a formal deep memory, everything happens in a present, hurtling forward and backward, in a "now here" that is nowhere. "Straw-Blond" ends with lines that affirm both its printed form—this is not a text in oral circulation—and "a great rooted" chestnut tree:

it came from Istanbul the hills of the Bosporus and settled in Paris
I don't know if it's still standing it would be about two hundred years old
I wish I could go shake its hand
I wish we could go lie in its shade the people who make the paper for this
*   book who set its type who print its drawings those who sell this*
*   book in their stores who pay money and buy it and look at it...*
(PNH 254-55)

The shade of the chestnut tree provides a resting place or landing for those who produce a book of poems and those who "look at it." It's also a resting place in Nazim's restless years and takes us back to an earlier poem, written for his then-wife, Münevver, from Sofia, her birth place:

The trees are still standing, the old benches dead and gone.
"Boris Park" is now "Freedom Park."
Under the chestnut I just thought of you
and you alone — I mean Memet,
just you and Memet, I mean my country…

1957
(PNH 190)

Nazim's compelling drive was to link the past to the present and the present to the future, to trace a necessary historical movement. Here the "historical process" is on a different scale, in a personal experience of time, as the past recedes farther back and the future rushes closer for the passenger on his "express" train to his destination, his "progress" measured by big, round, rail-station clocks.

Earlier, in *Human Landscapes from My Country*, trains had been emblems of the confusing anachronisms of modernization, as the very earth itself seemed to disappear under trains rushing over the terrain. The train that returns in the late poetry is a figure of the confusing anachronisms of a lifetime. "Things I Didn't Know I Loved," which takes place on a train and catalogues Nazim's newfound "loves," celebrates all that is "lost and found and lost again," and ends:

The train plunges on through the pitch-black night
I never knew I liked the night pitch-black
sparks fly from the engine
I didn't know I loved sparks
I didn't know I loved so many things and I had to wait until sixty to find it
out sitting by the window on the Prague-Berlin train watching the
world disappear as if on a journey of no return

(PNH 264)

I will close by reading a passage from "Straw-Blond," another poem riding the rails of a lifetime. This passage is remarkable for both its disorientation and its self-recognition in time and place after the poet's 40-year journey from his youth in revolutionary Russia to his less-than-utopian present in the USSR. The exiled poet at 59 meets his 19-year old self in a haunting scene at once intimate and coldly distant:

the clock tower on the Strastnoi Monastery rang midnight ...
that's where I met my nineteenth year
we recognized each other right away and we weren't surprised we tried
to shake hands
but our hands couldn't touch forty years stood between us
a North Sea frozen and endless
and it started snowing in Strastnoi now Pushkin Square
I'm cold especially my hands and feet
yet I have wool socks and fur-lined boots and gloves
he's the one without socks his feet wrapped in rags inside old boots his
                                                                hands bare
the world is the taste of a green apple in his mouth
songs go for miles and miles in his eyes and death measures a hand's-span
and he has no idea what will happen to him
only I know what will happen
because I believed everything he believes
I loved all the women he'll love
I wrote all the poems he'll write
I stayed in all the prisons he'll stay in
I passed through all the cities he will visit
I suffered all his pains
I slept all his nights dreamed all his dreams
I lost all he will lose
her hair straw-blond eyelashes blue

1961
(PNH 250-251)

Works Cited

- Bezirci, Asım. *Nazim Hikmet: Yaşamı, Şairliği, Eseri, Sanatı.* Istanbul; Çınar Yayınları, 1993.

- Erdinç, Fahri. *Kalkın Nazim's Gidelim.* Istanbul: Yordam Kitap, 1987.

- Hikmet, Nazim. *Kemal Tahir'e Mahpusaneden Mektuplar.* Ankara: Bilgi Yayınevi, 1968. Pp. 369, 368.

- *Poems of Nazim Hikmet.* Trans. Randy Blasing and Mutlu Konuk. New York: Persea Books, 2002. Cited in the text as PNH.

- Lewis, Bernard. *The Emergence of Modern Turkey.* 2nd Ed. Oxford: Oxford UP, 1968.

Dr. Mutlu Konuk Blasing is the author of The Art of Life (U of Texas Press, 1977), American Poetry (Yale, 1987), Politics and Form in Postmodern Poetry (Cambridge, 1995), and Lyric Poetry: The Pain and the Pleasure of Words (Princeton, 2007). She has published articles on Emerson, Whitman, James, Eliot, Pound, O'Hara, Bishop, Merrill, and others. She is the translator, with Randy Blasing, of Nazim Hikmet's work into English, and has published eight volumes of translations. The latest are Nazim Hikmet: Human Landscapes from My Country (Persea, 2002) and Poems of Nazim Hikmet (Persea, 2002). Blasing's research interests include American poetry, modern poetry, modernist and postmodernist poetics, poetic theory, lyric poetry, and translation theory.

*Tenth Annual
Nâzım Hikmet Poetry Competition*

Poetry Selection Committee

(In alphabetical order)

Greg Dawes (see page 27)

Erdağ Göknar (see page 36)

Rachel Richardson, NEA Fellow and Wallace Stegner Fellow, is the author of two books of poetry, *Copperhead* and *Hundred-Year Wave*. Her poems have appeared in the *New York Times* and many magazines, and she has been awarded the Stegner and National Endowment for the Arts Fellowship. She teaches at the University of San Francisco and directs the literary arts center Left Margin LIT in Berkeley, California.

Winners

(In alphabetical order)

Hawk

Blood on the snow,
a hawk, still as stone
on frozen ground,
its talons embedded
in gray pigeon-flesh.

Its scimitar beak
picks feathers so fast,
a new one's in the air
before the last one
hits the ground.

Feathers spin in their last
flight, away from the pigeon's
bare skin, sleek as porcelain.

The hawk's work is steady
as hunger, meticulous as need,
understandable as my grandmother
pulling feathers off the scalded
turkey by the handfuls.

I step forward and the hawk
flies up effortlessly
to the nearest tree, dangling
the dead, pendulous
weight of the pigeon.

Perched on a low branch,
it clutches the pigeon
against the limb.
Feathers sail down.
I catch one in my hand,
soft as a snowflake,
curved like a talon.

Peter Blair

Walking Market Square After Reading
    The Little Flowers of St. Francis

An idea eats at me, inside
my reflection in a plate-glass
bar window. A suited man

at an outdoor table munches
in the shade of a brick cornice.
He pays and walks out

into a dream of ants:
buildings, stories
stacked high into empty

air. Why do we labor
boxed in our own locked
glass? If Francis' dream

had worked: no land wars,
only a beautiful
poverty, a different city--

no guns, or me gritting
my mandibles. A burly cop
strolls; businessmen laugh

Peter Blair

over corned beef and foreign
beer, self-assured as hawks.
A man dripping rags

holds a sandwich board:
*Silent Wi-fi Is Controlling
Your Mind,* and shuffles

toward me, his hand out. I give him
a dollar because an idea
eats at me, that earth's a rock hotel

where the killing will go on
forever. *God bless*, he says.
Either way, we'll feed each other.

Peter Blair

Monongahela

1
Holes open up in the brown river.
Bubbling and gurgling, a carp
sucks frothy scum. A man
lives in the Fort Pitt Bridge,
enclosed by girders, crawls out
from a cardboard box bed.
I leave food for him.

2
At 22 below zero, the coldest day
on record, I step onto the ice,
break off a glassy shard, sharp
as a gleaming spike. Inside it,
elongated air bubbles blister
into human shapes. They float
like trapped bodies, arms splayed,
legs dragged down by gravity.

3
At flood stage, a punctured
oil can oozes slimy rainbows
into the water among barges
and dead rats. I love the bridges,
but I've known people who have jumped
from their thin, steel-cabled girders,
faces and arms disappearing
beneath green waves.

Peter Blair

Peter Blair's most recent book of poems is Farang, published by Autumn House Press. His book, Last Heat, won the 1999 Washington prize and was published by Word Works Press. Born in Pittsburgh, he has worked in a steel mill, a psychiatric ward, and spent three years in Thailand in the Peace Corps. He currently lives in Charlotte, NC, with his wife and son.

Michael Cirelli

Bucket List

2-2-17, Sultanahmet, Istanbul

I got the girl.
I got the girl that came from the girl.
One from *the one*, who's now two...
(She was also on the list.)
The last time we were here,
As the stray dogs nipped at
The stray laces of our boots
We wondered if we'd ever have a baby.
We bought a doll made of pieces
Of rug that was propped in the rug shop window
& voodooed a wish to the top
Of the minarets.
Today the seagulls still circle
Each spire of the Blue Mosque,
As if on a wire, and they wait
For the words that say: *God is Great.*
Last time, I didn't know how to pray
In Arabic, to the Allah of the Sultans,
& I vowed to come back one day
When I did. The Allah of the Popes
Had all my prayers back then,
Or the words at least—
& already: the Allah of this Charming Man
landed me in Birmingham,
& the Allah of the Siddhartha's
Brought me to Plum Village,
& the Allah of Cleaning Dishes
Taught me how to count my wishes,
& the Allah of Every Mistake
Helped me see straight...

Michael Cirelli

O what a life, to check off
Our bucket list twice!
At fajr, I'm the first one in the mosque,
So white and punctual that the muezzin
Is still sleeping. I polish the words
Over and over
In my mouth so as to not trip
On all the sharp points of them.
I feel like I'm preparing for an interview
With the one. But I already got
The one: she's in the only the place that's open now,
Drinking a coffee that is darker
Than midnight, sitting on a rug with our Aya.

Michael Cirelli

Eid al-Adha

It is hard to imagine
That you will be
Anything less than, like God,
To us. & that's not
Blasphemy, just
A slow intuition
That is gaining momentum
In our cosmology.
Here's a simple word: poop.
Here's a simple word: milk.
Here's some: red and black lumberjack
With the tutu to match.
How can we not deepen observance
As we tend to all of this?
Then there's: kindergarten.
Then there's: Elena of Avalor.
There's: tuition.
There will be tears said the Ocean.
The will be cuts said the Ice Rink, The Desk, The Swingset.
If He asked me to lay you out,
Your big lovely eyes fixed on the storm
Clouds in heaven,
I'd have to say *No*. I'd cleave the heavens
With that small sentence.
I imagine faith will become legless
In front of my child.

Michael Cirelli

I imagine faith will be
A girl in a bubble, & every
Word in there is sharp & Arabic:
Could sever a goat's neck in a stroke—
I've been memorizing new prayers
For nearly two years now.
Here's a word: fumbling.
& another: Insha'Allah.
I've saved a soft spot
In the middle of my forehead, like
A third eye, ready for
The chaffing. Me and your mother
Are mourning a little,
All that we will lose, when we gain
This new devotion.

Michael Cirelli

Becoming Un-single in the Miraculous Light

Walking through
The streets of Istanbul,
Coveting our neighbor's
Babies, we bought dolls
For the unfertilized egg.
We ate pomegranate,
& fish roe, slathered mayo
on everything and kept
Tabs on her cycle
Like we were puppeteers of the moon.
The months came and went
& we prayed for the blood to stop.
Forget all that now: wife's
Full blown, ready to float away.
Everything that took so
Long—is suddenly sudden
Death overtime.
The death of spooning.
The death of the spare bedroom.
The death of rational parents.
What does it feel like? they ask.
It feels like loss, like becoming
Un-single, even if we're married.
What are you thinking about?
The death of sleeping in.
The death of brunch.
The death of surfing all day long.
The death of writing?...how the fishing
lines hang from the Galata
Like the underside
Of a piano. I'm thinking, plotting
How to pull this all off with Aya in tow—
My wife's body is already dilating,
Quickly opening up like the mouth
Of a silver fish gasping for air.
Soon we will be hitched,
Our daughter pulling us to a place
That can only be described
In multiples & multitudes.

Michael Cirelli

Michael Cirelli is the author of four collections of poetry, most recently *The Grind* (Hanging Loose Press 2014). In 2008, he founded the National Youth Poet Laureate Program, that names local and national Youth Poet Laureates across the country.

Laura Grothaus

Proof

Proof of teeth is baby's gums
Proof of baby's gums is baby's mouth
Proof of baby's mouth is laugh
Proof of laugh is trust
Proof of trust is gamble
Proof of gamble is coin
Proof of coin is moon
Proof of moon is night
Proof of night is winter
Proof of winter is frost
Proof of frost is ghost
Proof of ghost is story
Proof of story is loneliness
Proof of loneliness is hunger
Proof of hunger is teeth

What you remember of the rock

Dark, dank, dizzying girl,
come out of the water, come out
of the moss. Trick-tongued
girl, wily and riled girl, girl
of white branch, of speckled
bark, girl with tender bows, with
thunder gloves, with jade
in her eyes, stone girl
coated with flies, itching
girl who has forgotten
all she was, remember
you sat on a rock and saw
the purple world all around you,
mountains in every direction,
ruddy laurel pinpricked pink,
pools of resting water
flecked black with tadpoles.
You dipped your finger in.
This is important.
Remember, you were there
to watch the world slide
into blue and it was not easy
to climb up, your heart
in your stomach, how hard
the stone was,
girl with raw feet,
sappy, sore, and oozing girl,
swarm of limbs, gentling yourself
through your own thoughts, jamming
foot after foot into crag,
straight up. You climbed and did not stop
until all around you was the wide world,
gnarled and waiting, only half waiting.
You must remember the way
it didn't even move,
didn't even look up, so certain
you would make it.

Laura Grothaus

The Selkie

shed her seal skin in the ocean,
peeled it off easy as a boiled tomato's,
to comb her hair
with human hands. Her body was

seamless and silken, milk's blister,
translucent with salt, shins glistened
loose light around her feet,
her hands, a dark thicket,

her inky mouth gritted
with laughter. I listened for her
after the sound had stopped.

All seals took on a glow.
Black butter eyes allured,
an aquarium smell enticed. The selkie knew
what kind of girls watched the sea like that,

let the rocks bite their toes.
Girls who had learned sweetness
to get by, who wore out their nights
with apologies.

So this was not the story of a fisherman
locking a seal's skin in a chest. This was revision
like shore is revised: sand transcribed
by tide, woman into seal into women.

She let me stroke the faint whiskers
above her lips, her dappled spine,
rough knees, hair like oil slick.

My feet tangled
with kelp, my hands
in the foam at her hips.

Waves slurred against our chests,
briny and whining.
      The tide caught in our mouths,
      did not stop rising.

Laura Grothaus

Laura Grothaus lives in Baltimore. This past year, her work was nominated for a Pushcart. Current projects include a book of poetry and drawings and a collection ghost stories as told by her father.

Rushda Rafeek

Love in Khyber

In Khyber, you leapt across the forehead
of hills wider than a martyr's gasp
for the corona of *nargis* torching her palm.
Qudsia, celestial one, implacable — when
your shoulders searched her snowfall mothering
a cloud of doves upon the mosque amidst dark
mulberry plumes. The augury you heard
was a dream's cry. In the feral of eye, in the wings
of a heart's commotion, you who crooned soft
towards the calyxed crescent of her arms,
you who became *dhikr* immortal, orphic saffron
bulbs raining upon wretched crusades — the tears
long as Indus past poppy fields awash in rays
limned warm and sun-drunk, you whose finger
rivered like catamaran on her mouth-filled body
sung slow of saint *alifs* until you were a lost drop.

Rushda Rafeek

Taṇhā / Desire

Follow the chants: a Tibetan's breath
turns to deities of snow. You navigate

silk route maps on his *ngapa* — drop by
drop constellated with *mala* beads. In blood

a shepherd's sojourn returns as though one
pressed miracles shaping the weep of his ancient

bones swollen with sutra. To devote means
let a tall pine's kiss tinkle my body. Learn rebirth.

Learn it mild as morning until doves illuminate
a sleepy monastery. There's enough silence to tuck in

as I lie next to you disrobing a lunar on the floor,
dervish spherule of obeah ample as avalanche

each time we convulse to beaten cymbals. Each rhythm
in floods flinching cold carnal, cosmic, complete.

Rushda Rafeek

City of the Moon

For Hatem, Palestine (2017)

Your asmar myrrh salams the air
of a city mountain. City of the moon,
embrocated hot and forlorn above janazah domes.
I watch you pull down heaven full with children
30 miles of rocket launch, 30 miles of refugee
camps, 30 miles of your tongue gone lost
in the mail, torn to shreds before they reached her.
The way you tell this rustles sleepless nights
of a lover in cuffs – a century's guilt, silence
after silence on lips pink with season. One day
God handed olives to a field she had wept in,
away from nemesis, rogue all hellion they who
snitch. *Behind you habibti!* you rode the wind
of Intifada then, halfway on the other side
where heliotropes survived on their knees;
homeless hopes, parting the brocade of her ovule
angel-heavy, bullet-solved.

Rushda Rafeek

Rushda Rafeek is currently based in Sri Lanka. Her work has appeared in numerous journals including a Pushcart Prize nomination and shortlisted for the Wasafiri New Writing Prize (2017)

Anya Russian

In Memoriam

Here on the edge of town
where civilization grits her teeth
we squirm as if caught for the first time
in an indecent act: the wild flowers quiver
a string of hints across the lap,
the bamboo trees creak an eerie
recollection from their long-stalked throats.
In the clutch and release
of the butterflies' wings—
the stroke of a brush against paper,
an elemental gesture
reminds of the pedal of youth
still intact.
                Even the mountains that brood
for months over the city's stubborn factory
seem nearly reachable now,
folded nicely like the pleats of a skirt.
Thank the orange-rimmed clouds
for sealing this hour,
so frail in flight, in ponds
where rice breed next to roadsides
for the next season, startling
the landscape with chartreuse notes.
Envy that force of intrusion,
like a day's wide-brimmed
hat tipped towards you
or an old yearning restored—
some memories remain
pure as the question
in the doe's round eyes, resolute
as a gun-barrel aimed at the heart.

Anya Russian

In the Lagoon

Silver fish give arrow
to the unsung horizon.
It could be a flock of sparrows
single file against the frigid cold;
how it protects its contraband,
the invisible temptation to flee.

Today nothing can be seen—
only the fletched pieces
of a tarnished profile.

A makeshift peer
no longer worth the wind's rebuke
quakes slightly, like a turtle
surfacing news of a place
far beyond grasp.

Ask the mangroves of their labor;
they extract but a tangled reflection
from the water's jester— too humble
or too bold to defy Archimedes.

   A body inside a body—
  which one contains the other?

The moon's stark shutter will not
hault the fisherman's vaults
churned by the same livid alphabet
that crafts the night's Braille
and the red pulse of a lone boat
gives stark note to what
unseen is no less stealthy.

  Who knows the moral of the story—
too many have chased too long after that kite
   having forgotten
the urge to run is what we hold on to.

Anya Russian

Yes— the horizon
is a clean break.
Or more like a palimpsest
as the broken sand
sinks again,
recollecting its armor— the shattered
efforts of hours washed ashore—
small deaths whose pocket-sized irony
you will never fully grasp.

Today nothing can be seen—
the spright grasses whistle
of an intimate fire
and the sea reads as silk
unafraid of its seams
as a heron watches suspiciously,
its white resolute against the slow
tugging testimony beneath,

                it watches
me

who knows nothing
but calls it
calm.

Geography Lessons

Wednesday. The sky razed
down to a bare blue scrim,
the leaves hardly a rumor of fall.

A bell tower scolds
pleating the summer's drone.
A bell tower scolds
and even the insects
grow persuasive.

The ear attempts to find the rail
between sound and warning,
to pry the iron brow
with a honeysuckle's jest.

But a widowed note
will multiply into thousands
like the scaffold of dew that lingers
on the brittle grass still unmasked
by the sun's portrait.
It bows like the present tense
adhering to an ephemeral alphabet.

The sky knows better the price of waking,
the murals that slip in and out of grasp. Each day
redeeming this somnambulant town,
giving ode to the brick alters of its universities
and shrillness to the quaint suburbs;
capturing leisurely faces in hopeful storefronts,
the still life in front yards: plastic ducks, hedges
allowed their rightful rebellion, and wind chimes
that waken empty porches preoccupied with a beer
can where familiar flags, like the kudzu, survey
how much likeness can be held in reach.

Anya Russian

The sky knows better the price of waking — the
million ways to retreat with runners along railroad tracks
that still spite the city's shuffling hours into dark
and light — the same old story trading hands.

But the summer is content
with the fireflies' ventriloquy,
the azure of alleged verses.
The sun is just a mime threading
yesterday's ink through this one.

Even the blue jay carries on
in brass solitude
cajoling the old oak
trees reconciled to shadows.

The bell tower scolds
and even the sidewalk surrenders,
figures retire into circuitous geometries
leaving a trail of lost gestures —
a question to write oneself through.

Now imagine the pearl's solidarity
bred within a shell's ward
for years   never once
rattled by tide or tempted by
the mirror of a bloodshot dusk;
never once craning
for the earnest slope of a neck
or to shed its chapel for the salt
tinged thrills of a thespian wind.

Maybe that is wisdom —
a solemn pact with oneself,
a language with no proof or logic
but the sun's gambled revelations —
the hour's rhyme that carves a rift
between destination and reason
and the mind's lonely atlas.

Anya Russian

Anya Russian (Greensboro, NC) is a creative nomad who has lived and traveled in 11 countries and speaks three languages. She has a natural tendency to reinvent herself. Trained in classical and contemporary dance, Anya has performed on stages worldwide and collaborated with artists of diverse disciplines. She has also slept on dirt floors and survived altitude sickness while backpacking solo through Asia for 8 months. Anya is intrigued by the space between people, languages, cultures, and landscapes and the infinite ways we try to span it. You may find her translating poetry from the Spanish language, working with the immigrant and refugee community, stretching outside on a sunny day, rock climbing, or writing poetry, which distills her lesser known penchant for the simple things that matter most in life.

Deema K. Shehabi

Ghazal: A Lover's Quarrel with the World

History gallops over the margins of your page, what's a story, but its plural all over the world?
Arabic lulls ageless in your ears, but to you what most matters is temporal in this world.

The Sheikh with a gold pen in his pocket, the girl lathering her father's head with musk,
and you — pearling over Whitman's poems — all have a lover's quarrel with the world.

A riddle of childhood loss soaks the rearview mirror in an Arizona desert,
and you drive past the unsaid but ignite nothing immoral in this world.

When you put your head down to grass to gaze at the fallen sparrow,
your eyes met rest in its body and what's silent became oral in the world.

The child, splintered with too many voices, hears only yours,
and her paths, dismantled of sound, light up murals of this world.

A sweet theft, a heavy hour of grief, and a ghazal posturing for friendships
that never fade, vine-leafed gardens in which we hide against the perils of this world.

Her face is a balm against fracture; the light on her moon is a cheek you return to,
and you say time has no stride against her flushed lips, flickering corals of this world.

How else to bundle this dark where pillow meets dream,
and the one acquainted with the night rises like an immortal of this world?

Deema K. Shehabi

Pines at Shuhada Cemetery, Beirut

After frames of incense,
porous yellow sponges,
salt-sea jugs, myrrh for flight,
we flush your ears out,
pour cool musk water
over your head,
softly untie your throat,
and smooth the dandelions
on your blue-lit chest
with muslin cloth.
I can hear your voice
over this syntax
of supplications
rising above pendulous
jacarandas, and Palestine
sunbirds upraising twilight
over the mountains,
but how do I bear
these pine trees swinging
low in this cemetery
named for fighters
who sought refuge
against death's punctuality,
or these heavily-bundled children
with their bleached-out smiles
skipping barefoot
over white marble slabs?
Their business is to wash
graves, and offer words,
moths knocking
on windows at night:
please, please,
may you
live long
in his place.

Deema K. Shehabi

Once when I was a child
you said it seems
that I had already lived
long and come so far,
but that there was no shame
in turning back.
We were in America,
and it was a day
of our first leave-taking
from one another.
If America became my home,
I was swallowed whole,
and standing in this cemetery
only means that you are buried,
and I am an orphan.
But with no remorse
or shame, let us turn back here —
and stroke the sun's hair,
leaving these needles
for other souls.

Deema K. Shehabi

Robert Frost at the Alumni Garden

October's stealth light
leavens the skin
then molts into Nuttall Oaks.

No preamble to a scream
interrupts the glistening rub
of downward wings

except for the hum
of poets acquainted with one another.
The one made of bronze

cools the day's fire from their breaths,
so that news of faraway
places lifts briefly,

and in this afternoon
there are no bodies scraped
from deformed fans in Kashmir

nor children gushing out
of cemented pipes in Gaza.
For a small wrinkle,

the women of Tahrir
caress dragonflies with their fingertips
and flood the tank's long arm

with bracelets of jasmine.
The fluted fountain
in the courtyard

stands only as an ode
to timelessness,
but not shadows

as we elide
over an inscription
with a watchman in it.

Deema K. Shehabi

Deema K. Shehabi is the author of *Thirteen Departures from the Moon*, co-author of *Diaspo/Renga* with Marilyn Hacker and co-editor with Beau Beausoleil of *Al-Mutanabbi Street Starts Here*, for which she received the NCBR Book Recognition Award. Her work has been widely published in anthologies and literary journals.

Honorable Mentions

(In alphabetical order)

Chris Abbate

Batting Cage

Each time he swung and missed
it was as if his father
had died suddenly again;
his body unwound
in a posture of spent effort.

And the times he connected –
the sting of the bat in his spleen –
was some recompense for every year
he had stayed home
to care for his mother.

But there was something feeble
about the violence of his hits –
his loosened chin,
the ache in his arms,
the ball slackening
into the netting as if to say
it had been hit harder
by more imposing men,
fatherless men too,
before falling
to the batting cage floor
and gazing back at him
with its red-stitched smirk.

Chris Abbate

Neighborhood Men

Neighborhood men talk in driveways, over the hoods of SUVs,
they talk as if they need a piece of steel between them.

They talk in clichés, spit consonants, curse like car engines starting.
They stop their lawnmowers to talk, fold themselves over to pull a stray weed.

They talk about the thing they just bought, how much they saved,
they like to compare their stuff to your stuff, explain why you need the stuff they have.

Neighborhood men talk like tools in the garage, potential energy,
they talk about what they will do someday when they have the time.

They talk about tomorrow or next week, they say *we should* to each other
as in going out for a beer or playing golf some Saturday, but until then

they will hang like shovels in perfect rows. They will be reliable and stiff.
They will wake up, get dressed and drive to work, and at the end of the day

they will pull into the driveway, go inside, turn on the news, and ponder
the hard lines of houses and yards and sidewalks, the ones the neighborhood

seemed to draw around them when they weren't paying attention.
They will think of ways to bend the lines into a shape they can describe,

the shape of diligence, of winches, and chain saws, and trees they used to climb,
one that resembles the question their wives are always asking,

the shape of contentment, a thought that vanishes somewhere between the alarm clock
and the shower, a shape they could fall in love with if only it had a name.

Chris Abbate

Killing The Fish

A fish in my tank
is dying of old age
of all things,
which makes this one unique;
having lived six years,
her underside sunken in now,
her body blemished,
fins like tattered flags
of surrender.
I want to save her
a shred of dignity –
as dignified as a net
and toilet can be –
but she eludes me;
whips her delicate
blue body
and slips between
stacks of slate.

The others will sense
her weakness
and will pick
at her without mercy.
I know –
I have endured high school,
job layoffs,
and family divorce.
I have seen how some of us eat
each other;
first the hands and arms,
then the stomach,
and finally the eyes.

The next morning
the fish wills herself
to the surface for food;

Chris Abbate

her miraculous little jaw
still hinging
open and closed.
She seems lost
in some aqueous eternity,
a flow she keeps secret.
She is at the center
of the universe;
as much as anything else,
as much as me.
And who's to say each of us isn't?
As if we knew where the center was.

Later, I slide
the net toward her again,
but she escapes.
This is as good as it gets,
she seems to say,
and I am hard pressed
to explain her grit.
God, let me be like that.

Chris Abbate

Chris Abbate's poetry has appeared in *Comstock Review*, *Timberline Review*, and *Chagrin River Review* among other journals. He has been nominated for the Pushcart Prize and a Best of the Net award, and was an honorable mention in the 2013 Nazim Hikmet Poetry Competition. Chris' first book of poetry, *Talk About God*, was published in 2017 by Main Street Rag. Chris works as a database programmer for a pharmaceutical company in Raleigh. He leads a local monthly poetry workshop, and he has served as a lead coach for *The First Tee* golf program since 2009. Originally from Hartford, CT, Chris resides in Holly Springs, NC with his wife. (chrisabbate.com)

Jen Arthur

Irma

All week, she left messages begging him to leave Miami,
to head further up the coast to stay with her,
but she hears nothing
but quiet in the birdless sky
as the winds begin sucking the ocean into the storm,
leaving the seabed dry,
the boats grounded.

She shutters the house,
brings in the striped patio furniture,
the potted rosemary, basil, and thyme
and checks her phone again,
knowing he won't call her back.
"My own son won't talk to me,"
she told her sister last Christmas.

She fills the bathtub with emergency water and
remembers Hurricane Andrew,
not long after his father left, when his four year old body
crumpled into hers in the closet, the wind peeling back
the roof like an orange rind.
Her chest hollowed over him as the house shook
and the trees ripped in two.

Now she prays for power,
lighting candles and hoping
not to have to use the expensive Alaskan salmon
she was saving.
Her mind goes to the storm surge
and all the water that comes rushing back
like memories
as she sits on the couch in the dark,
waiting for the wind and waves to bring him home.

Jen Arthur

Mother's Day

If you had walked the woods
with me on Mother's Day,
you'd have seen millions of dandelion seeds
floating in the air
like dust or cotton or feathers,
so many
it was as if the whole world had been wishing
their mothers back from the grave,
back from dementia,
wishing they had called home even once more,
wishing they could crawl back
inside their mothers to rest like nesting dolls.

Then I remembered Cheryl Strayed
wrote about swallowing some of her mother's ashes
and I don't blame her for this —
the tiny pebbles of bone sliding
down her throat,
gravelly dust settling
in the lines of her palms,
wishing
and keeping her mother
the only way she could.

Jen Arthur

Divorce Care

I don't know how my friend does planks
every day. She rises
at five in the morning, trying
to beat the day to its starting line.
It makes her feel whole to face the grave,
wrists aching, shoulders shaking,
toes curled back on their hinges.
Then her mind goes
to her three children, and her own warrior spirit,
and she is muscle and heart and blood,
fingers pressed into the earth,
her hands holding up the world.

Jen Arthur

Jen Arthur works in MBA admissions at North Carolina State University and is the owner of Jen Arthur Photography. Born and raised in Stuart, Florida, she graduated with a B.A. in English from Palm Beach Atlantic University and an MBA from Rollins College. Her work has appeared in *Living Waters Review*. She lives in Raleigh, NC, with her husband and daughter.

Jill A. Coyle

Old Barn in the Sunlight

The barn's old body is open
at the gable
the triangle precipice
transforms its heart-held space
into a sanctum of wood,
dust, and day

crooked boards loosely recline
propped against stronger planks
slouching now, but
this only serves
to let more life inside

wooden pegs lie askew
as if the searching wind
has pried the slabs apart
to peek into half-light

as when in the quiet dark
a patch of air is illuminated
from the side
and swimming in a shaft of light
the air we breathe
comes to life

flecks of detritus
mingled with mites and hay
bits of seeds, the scat of animals,
and what sloughs off of us
imperceptibly, all the time

breath passing across the threshold like a sieve
the world passes through this body

Jill A. Coyle

Closing the Distance

My small fingers barely strong enough to lift it
I twisted the handle of Grandpa's vice in the backyard shanty
Just to feel its weight

In the warm mustiness of young summer
The shack's open door let in no air

On a wooden floor made smooth
By years of soles shuffling the sawdust between silent walls
Grandpa worked beside me

His sharpened pencil marked measured increments on soft wood

I let the vice's handle plummet and turn like the hands of a clock

My loud iron clang rattled the rusty nails in the coffee can
On the window sill between us

With each turn I watched this old machine
Move gracefully
In stages

That iron embrace tightened around nothing
And kept closing the distance

Jill A. Coyle

Metal, wood, leather

My father kept his ax
in leather-

the metal blade in a leather case
stiff, worn, and cracked
it had a snap to snap it shut
tight, snug

Kept the metal bright, clean
and strong,
polished and scoured

by the hearts of logs
he split

In autumn, the thwack
and crack
echoed
through bare trees
filled the spaces
between
thin trunks

The way footsteps echo
through wooden pews
in a cathedral

When he halved a log often
the two pieces stood silent a moment
still connected
by smooth, pale strands
like sinews

until the two sides parted.

Jill A. Coyle

When he finished, we threw the logs
onto a pile together

My small hands in his leather gloves, I loved
the hollow sound of timber-

a smaller log meeting a larger
crosswise
and sliding
until it hit a niche
and stuck there.

Jill A. Coyle

Jill A. Coyle grew up in northeastern Pennsylvania where she developed a close affinity for nature that continues to influence her writing. She received a Ph.D. in Classical Studies from Duke University and later earned an M.A. in English from North Carolina State University. Jill lives on the edge of the Blue Ridge Mountains in upstate South Carolina and teaches English at Spartanburg Methodist College. Jill was awarded the Hub City Emrys Prize in poetry in 2015, and again in 2017. Her poems have appeared in Blueline, Avocet, Main Street Rag, The Independent Weekly, Raleigh Review, and elsewhere.

Maximilian Heinegg

EASTER AFTERNOON

When my wife slid the daunting needle into her childless
sister's side, we kept our ease quiet. Now their trinity
ranges loud across the yard, & it's a blessed stretch

to walk their youngest toward the egg, barely hidden
& gold at the feet of Jesus, the two-foot concrete statue
they found face down, lifted & now treat as auspicious.

If there was no hunt, faith would still take some finding,
behind the wetland, more a swamp beside a coop the foxes
emptied, one layer at a time. In the shell of my own miracle,

I stand by the Son in the same bodhisattva pose, hand open,
the symbolic heart pinned on his robe & the cross, victorious
standard, but his right arm's broken, in the pine needles.

I'd take what's left of his hand, but I carry the cherub's
basket & protect her forgotten boon of candy, plastic.
She targets the miniature castle & her instant siege

succeeds, the sweetest clutch. In unseasonable heat,
the garden's fake owl scares the fruit-thieves from theirs,
but the North Shore tomatoes now grow until November.

Denial's as ubiquitous as rebirth, the grass a deep green
overnight. For us, long summers & longer falls, but when
we've shaded the earth, who will move the boulder? After

Good Harbor, the boy cuts us cucumbers with a butter knife,
& my better's lovely, bare-kneed in April, musing whose birth
is fairest. *Any, safely delivered.* My brother in law tells me, when

his is caught in brambles, how the Germans joyed at dawn, but
still set the children's gems in nettles. She plucks them off, so
eager each capture feels the first, no tears at the sight of thorns.

Maximilian Heinegg

GARLIC

I bury it face up
before the spring frost, so
each clove becomes a head,
as in Cadmus, where each seeded
dragon tooth erupts a warrior.

We clip & fry the scapes, but also wait
to pull the hard-necks & dry
them in the shed. Sharpening
as divided, or coddled
in foil, pulp gold for our bread,

but charred in oil-smoke, an insult-
lingering
lily of the pyramids,
fifteen pounds for a slave,
scorodon to the Greeks,

poultice to a centurion,
or chewed to whet a killing
lust, & afterwards, felt
a sifting in the blood. *Allium-*
those legions called for it,

after salting the fields, planting
courage in the doomed Celts.
Then Alaric found the Roman gates
& the long ships went both ways
on the whale-road, as the old Germans sang-

so the Angles named the island England
& the sea-axe named its tribe-
their double-tongue mothers mine,
whose keen war-eyes saw the *spear-
leek,* nearly a weapon in the ground.

Maximilian Heinegg

THE BODHISATTVA OF COMPASSION

1.
Though shade rests on the branch
        of her sister, & the trunk
of her mother, she looks only for the tall flower

of friendship in the garden of strangers
        where the rocky soil splits, harbors
bee-balm, wild mint, columbine.

None to assist me in the weathering
        away, Boston's three modes: cloud
fickle, *wicked* sun, & *bullshit*.

2.
I rouse my phone again, hoping for my own
        acceptance, but it's blind feelers
& the clamor of first-world problems:

broken front step bricks to stagger
        litigious mailmen, lurching Halloween
children. The house as body frames the narrative

of alignment, as around, so within,
        the basement's disused weights,
each muscle waiting on maintenance.

3.
We weave to the museum with the genius of satellites,
        road by road we avoid *dukkha*,
by the Rose Garden, spy the fens that shield the flesh

& its brevities, the courts where I could scarcely gather
        a rebound, across the small pond & bridge -
six summers I taught *The Dark Thirty* & myths to the class

of Dorchester & Roxbury - welcome as water
        despite my whiteness. We shared the respite,
turning pages whose music few depend upon.

4.
Past the giant infant faces, we note the headset set, avoid Gauguin,

Maximilian Heinegg

          a bastard, & linger on Degas, frightened by Van Gogh's
swollen streams, house beams bloated, fields of vitriol,

the presence pressing in. We follow the girls
          past Virgil & Dante, marble Byron, to Athena,
my childhood goddess, the skull-splitting mix

of strength & wisdom, a better warrior than War-
          to the Singer Sargent ceilings,
& the Bodhisattva of Compassion.

5.
I stand before her stone hands wishing
          for my daughters & each stony face
weathered into weakness, a ready fragment

to tender dust for peace. Before the sage,
          nothing myself, I glimpse the veil
of our trials, separations.

I cleave sorrow closer, leave it no room
          to escape, & follow what passes
for the soul, on to sameness.

Maximilian Heinegg

Maximilian Heinegg's poems have appeared in The Cortland Review, Tar River Poetry, Columbia Poetry Review, December Magazine, and Crab Creek Review, among others. He lives in Medford, MA, where he has taught English in the public schools for 20 years. He is also a singer-songwriter and adapter of classic poems, and his records can be heard at
www.maxheinegg.com

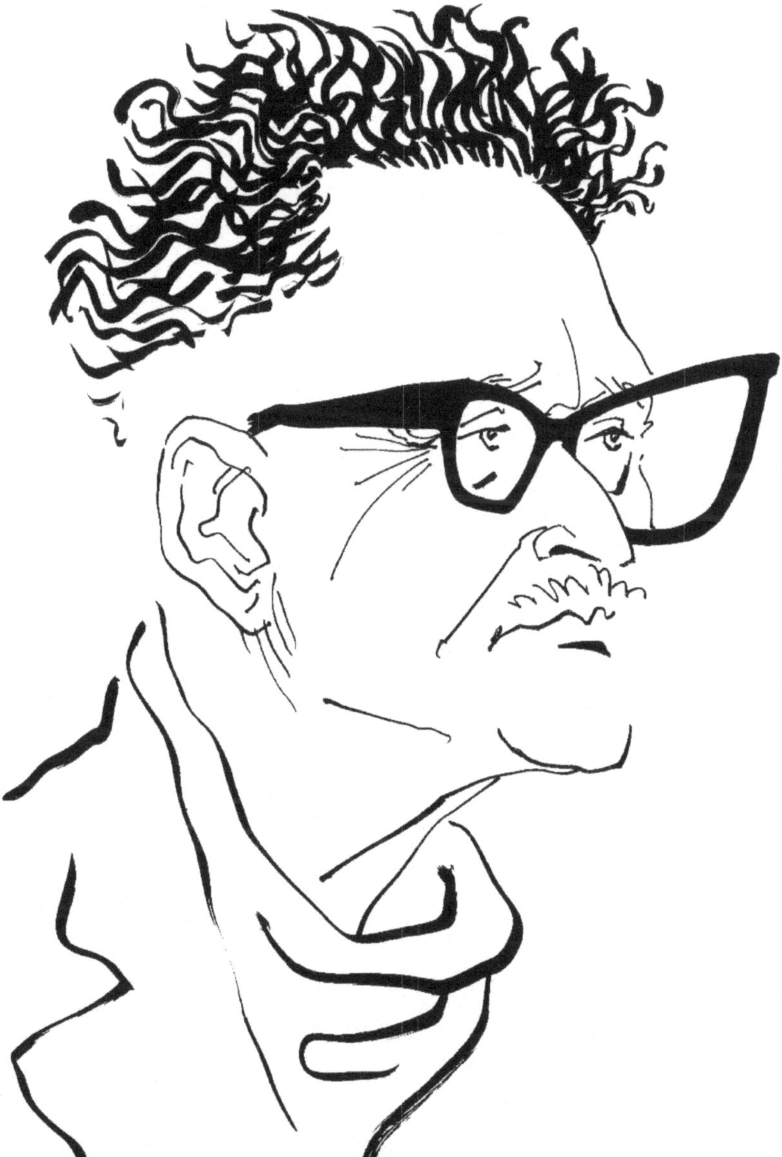
14 Ekim 2000

Made in the USA
Columbia, SC
21 March 2018